I0015335

Comparative Study of C++, Java and PHP

Chandrakant Naikodi, Suresh L & Badrinath G Srinivas

Comparative Study of C++, Java and PHP

Published by White Falcon Publishing
No. 335, Sector - 48 A
Chandigarh - 160047

ISBN - 978-1-943851-69-0

First Edition,
Copyright © 2016 Chandrakant Naikodi, Suresh L & Badrinath G Srinivas
All rights reserved

No part of this publication may be reproduced, stored in a retrieval system, or transmitted, in any form or by means electronic, mechanical, photocopying, or otherwise, without prior written permission of the Author.

Requests for permission should be addressed to Chandrakant Naikodi, Suresh L & Badrinath G Srinivas (chandrakant.naikodi@yahoo.in).

ABOUT AUTHOR

- Dr. Chandrakant Naikodi

  Dr. Chandrakant Naikodi is presently working as a Project Leader in MNC., Bangalore, India. He has received B.E. degree from the Visvesvaraya Technological University, Karnataka, India in 2004, and M.E. and Ph.D(CSE) degrees from Bangalore University, India in 2006 and 2014 respectively. His research interests include Computer Networks, MANETs, WSN, Programming Languages, Big Data and Databases. He has published many research papers in referred International Journals and Conferences. Also, he is the author of five technical books titled "C:Test Your Aptitude" and "1000 Questions and Answers in C++" published by Tata Mc-Graw Hill and other technical books titled "Programming in C and Data Structure", "Managing Big Data" and "Introduction to Computing and Problem Solving" by Vikas Publication which are widely used in both industry and academia. He has published over 50 papers in International Conferences and Journals.

- Dr. Suresh L

  Dr. Suresh L, Principal of CiTech, is ambitious and has been an eminent achiever throughout his service. He has over 24 years of teaching and administration experience. He is a source of inspiration for all the Cambrians, both faculties and students. He is a path setter for the development of both students and faculties. He is instrumental in conducting all college activities successfully. Apart from being a able leader, he is recognized as an eminent teacher. He is a member of Board of Studies / Examiners for various universities and autonomous Institutions. He has visited many countries like Singapore, Malaysia, Poland, Australia, UAE and Greece for academic pursuits. He gave Key Note address in the IEEE conference at Singapore. He is a Life member of ISTE and CSI and member of IEEE. He has published over 50 papers in National and International Conferences and Journals. His current areas of interest include Data mining, Database Management Systems, Cloud Computing and Big Data. He had been a member of recruitment committees and resource person for many corporate companies.

- Dr. Badrinath G. Srinivas

  Dr Badrinath G. Srinivas is presently working as a Development Manager in Samsung India Electronics Pvt Ltd, India. He has received B.E. degree from the Visvesvaraya Technological University, Karnataka, India in 2003. He has received M.E. and Ph.D. degrees from Bangalore University, India in 2005 and Indian Institute of Technology Kanpur, India in 2012 respectively. His research interests include Biometrics, Pattern recognition, Computer Vision, Large Data Classification and Indexing for efficient searching, Human Computer Interface, Graphical and Gesture based authentication techniques robust to shoulder surfing and Wireless Networks. He has published many conference and journal articles in premium forums. He has also published four patents on authentication techniques robust shoulder security and human interface for audio files.

PREFACE

- Nowadays programmers are encouraged or gets opportunity to learn more than one Object Oriented Languages which include C++, JAVA and PHP, in such cases this book gives an wonderful learning capability in short time by comparing all the features of Languages. We used C++11, Java6/7 and PHP5.4/5.5 for compiling C++, JAVA and PHP programs respectively. This book concentrates on comparing Basic Language features, Frequently Asked Questions, and Aptitude Questions with syntaxes and examples wherever required. The author will appreciate the suggestions or feedback from the readers and users of this book, kindly communicate via email addresses chandrakant.naikodi@{yahoo.in,gmail.com,facebook.com}.

To Vaishnavi

Contents

Chapter 1

Introduction

C++(superset of C) is a computer language which is statically typed, free-form, multi-paradigm, compiled, general-purpose programming language. It is known as intermediate-level language which is a combination of both high-level and low-level language features.

Java is a computer language which is used for multi-purpose, concurrent, class-based, object-oriented computer programming language which derives much of its syntax from C and C++, but it has fewer low-level facilities than either of them.

PHP is a computer language, PHP stands for Hypertext Preprocessor, that is a widely-used for multi purpose, it is a open source scripting language which is executed on the server side.

1.1 OVERVIEW COMPARISON OF C++, JAVA AND PHP

Features	C++	Java	PHP
Pointers	Supports	Not supports	Supports references
Preprocessor	Supports	Does not supports.	Implicitly does it, processes the code before execution or compilation.
Operator overloading.	Supports	Not supports	Limited
Compiled and/or Interpreted	Compiled	Compiled and interpreted	Interpreted
Multiple inheritance	Supports	Can achieve through interface.	Can be achieved.
Structures or unions	Includes	Not includes	Not includes
Annotations	Supports	Supports	Supports
Global variables	Supports	Not supports but you can achieve through it by static variable.	Supported, GLOBAL keyword can be used.

1

Header files	It has header files.	It does not have but have *import*.	The *include* statement includes and evaluates the specified file.
Automatic type conversion	Does perform.	Does not perform.	Does perform.
Constructors	Yes	Yes	Yes
Destructors	It is allowed	It does not allow but you can use *finalize()* function.	It is allowed through _destruct().
The *delete* operator	It has *delete* operator.	It does not have *delete* operator.	It does not have *delete* operator.
Templates	Supports	Does not support.	Does not support.
Default member access	Package level access (more *public*).	*private*	*public*
Portability	Not fully portable	Yes, it is platform-independent.	Yes, it is platform-independent.
Speed	Faster compare to JAVA.	Slow compare to C++, because of 2 steps to run a application(compile and interpret).	Slow compare to C++.
Pass by value and pass by reference.	Both supports.	Pass by value.	Pass by value.
Common root object	Not achievable.	Yes it has, i.e., Object class	Not achievable
Built in Exception class hierarchy.	Not available	Available	Available
Runtime polymorphism.	Not supports	Supports	Supports
System dependent	Yes	No	
Supporting object serialization.	Serializes to a stream.	Serializes to a stream or to XML.	Serializes to a stream.
Interfaces	Not supported	Supported	Not supported
Scope of class members	*public, protected,* and *private*	*public, private, protected,* and default (package)	Only default public scope
Security	Yes	Yes	Yes
Multithreading	No	Yes	Yes
Automatic garbage collection	No	Yes	Yes
Function overloading	Yes	Yes	No
Function overriding	Yes	Yes	Yes
break, continue statements	Yes	Yes	Yes
Loops	Yes	Yes	Yes

Destructors	Yes	No	Yes
Few data types are common	Yes	Yes	Yes
Method overloading	Supported	Supported	Supported
Abstract classes and methods	Supported	Supported	Supported
Exception handling	Achieved through *try, catch,* and *throw*	Achieved through *try,catch, throw* and *finally.*	Achieved through *try, catch* and *throw*

1.2   LANGUAGE ARCHITECTURE

C++ Language Architecture	Java Language Architecture	PHP Language Architecture

```
+-------------------+
|   Source Code     |
| (e.g., hello.cpp) |
|                   |
+-------------------+
         ⇓
+-------------------+
|                   |
|   Compiler        |
+-------------------+
         ⇓
+-------------------+
|                   |
|   Object Code     |
| (e.g., hello.obj) |
+-------------------+
         ⇓
+-------------------+
|                   |
|   Linker          |
+-------------------+
         ⇓
+-------------------+
|                   |
|   Machine code    |
+-------------------+
         ⇓
+-------------------+
|       OS          |
|   +---------+     |
|   |  CPU    |     |
|   +---------+     |
+-------------------+
```

```
+-------------------+
|   Source Code     |
| (e.g., Hello.java)|
|                   |
+-------------------+
         ⇓
+-------------------+
|                   |
|   Java Compiler   |
+-------------------+
         ⇓
+-------------------+
|                   |
|   Byte Code       |
| (e.g., Hello.class)|
+-------------------+
         ⇓
+-------------------+
|Java Virtual Machine|
| +---------------+ |
| |      OS       | |
| | +---------+   | |
| | |  CPU    |   | |
| | +---------+   | |
| +---------------+ |
+-------------------+
```

```
+-------------------+
|   Source Code     |
| (e.g., hello.php) |
|                   |
+-------------------+
         ⇓
+-------------------+
|   Opcode          |
|   Compiler(Zend)  |
+-------------------+
         ⇓
+-------------------+
|                   |
|   Opcode Optimizer|
|   Opcode Cache    |
+-------------------+
         ⇓
+-------------------+
|                   |
|   Opcode Executor |
+-------------------+
         ⇓
+-------------------+
|        OS         |
|   +---------+     |
|   |  CPU    |     |
|   +---------+     |
+-------------------+
```

1.3   PROGRAM STRUCTURE IN C++, JAVA AND PHP

C++ Language Structure	Java Language Structure	PHP Language Structure
| ```
+------------------+
|   Header file    |
|   Declaration    |
+------------------+

        ⇓

+------------------+
|    Global        |
|    Declaration   |
+------------------+

        ⇓

+------------------+
| Class Declaration|
| and Method       |
| Definition       |
+------------------+

        ⇓

+------------------+
|   Main function  |
+------------------+

        ⇓

+------------------+
|   Method         |
|   Definition     |
+------------------+
``` | ```
+--------------------+
| Documentation      |
| Section(suggest)   |
+--------------------+

         ⇓

+--------------------+
| Package Statement  |
| (optional)         |
+--------------------+

         ⇓

+--------------------+
| Import Statements  |
|(optional)          |
+--------------------+

         ⇓

+---------------------+
| Interface Statements|
| (optional)          |
+---------------------+

         ⇓

+---------------------+
| Class Definitions   |
| (optional)          |
+---------------------+

         ⇓

+---------------------+
| Main Method         |
| (Mandatory)         |
+---------------------+
``` | ```
+--------------------+
|   Includes Code    |
+--------------------+

         ⇓

+--------------------+
|  Define Globals    |
+--------------------+

         ⇓

+--------------------+
|  Helper functions  |
+--------------------+

         ⇓

+--------------------+
| Main script logic  |
+--------------------+
``` |
```

1.4   SAMPLE PROGRAM IN C++, JAVA AND PHP

C++	Java	PHP
```Program Name:\nHelloWorld.cpp\n#include <iostream.h>\nint main ()\n{\n cout << "Hello World!";\n return 0;\n}```	```Program Name:\nHelloWorld.java\npublic class HelloWorld {\npublic static void main\n(String[] args)\n{\nSystem.out.\nprintln("Hello World!");\n}\n}```	```Program Name:\nHelloWorld.php\n<?php\n echo "Hello World!";\n?>```

Chapter 2

Data Types

A data type is type to identify a classification of data or a set of data with values having predefined characteristics.

The variable of different data type like character, wide character, integer, floating point, double floating point, boolean etc is required to store various information. Here, variables are used to reserve the memory locations to store values. Using data type of a variable, the OS allocates memory and decides what can be stored in the reserved memory.

Primitive data types in C++ are, Boolean i.e, bool, Character i.e, char, Integer i.e, int, Floating point i.e, float, Double floating point i.e, double, Valueless i.e, void and Wide character i.e, wchar_t.

In Java, there are 8 primitive data types are available, they are, Integer types (Does not allow decimal places) i.e, byte, short, int, long; Rational Numbers(Numbers with decimal places) i.e, float, double; characters i.e, char; conditional i.e, boolean.

In PHP scripts, data stored in variables and PHP can work with different data types, e.g, a whole number is said to have an integer data type, while a string of text has a string data type. Scalar data can hold a single value. The PHP6 data types are, integer(A whole number), float(A floating point number), string(sequence of characters), unicode(sequence of unicode characters), binary(sequence of binary (non-Unicode) characters), and boolean(either true or false). PHP uses dynamic data typing instead variables assume the type of the value currently contained in them, and can change their type to satisfy implicit casts and conversions.

Languages C++ and JAVA, we need to define the variable data types as well while declaring them but in PHP, we don't have to define the type of the variable while declaring it. Just give a variable any value. A variable may be evaluated with different values in certain situations, depending on what type it is at the time.

Java contains fixed sized data types, while all basic data types in PHP and C++ depends on the actual platform (machine architecture + operating system) the program is compiled for.

2.1 BASIC DATA TYPES

Data Type	C++		JAVA		PHP	
	Size	Default Value	Size	Default Value	Size	Default Value
bool	1byte	GV	NA	NA	NA	NA
boolean	NA	NA	1bit	false	SD	NS
char	1byte	GV	2bytes	'0000'	NA	NA
unsigned char	1byte	GV	NA	NA	NA	NA
signed char	1byte	GV	NA	NA	NA	NA
string	NA	NA	NA	NA	SD	NS
int	4bytes(CD/SD)	GV	4bytes	0	NA	NA
integer	NA	NA	NA	NA	SD	NS
unsigned int	4bytes(CD/SD)	GV	NA	NA	NA	NA
signed int	4bytes	GV	NA	NA	NA	NA
short	2bytes	GV	2bytes	0	NA	NA
short int	2bytes	GV	2bytes	0	NA	NA
unsigned short int	Range	GV	NA	NA	NA	NA
signed short int	Range	GV	NA	NA	NA	NA
long	4bytes(CD/SD)	GV	8bytes	0	NA	NA
long int	4bytes(CD/SD)	GV	NA	NA	NA	NA
signed long int	4bytes	GV	NA	NA	NA	NA
unsigned long int	4bytes	GV	NA	NA	NA	NA
float	4bytes	GV	4bytes	0.0	SD	NS
double	8bytes	GV	8bytes	0.0	NA	NA
long double	8bytes	GV	NA	NA	NA	NA
wchar_t	2/4 bytes	GV	NA	NA	NA	NA
byte	NA	NA	2bytes	0	NA	NA
array	NA	NA	NA	NA	SD	NS
object	NA	NA	NA	NA	SD	NS
resources	NA	NA	NA	NA	SD	NS
NULL	NA	NA	NA	NA	NT	NT
void	PT/ED	ED	NA	NA	SD	NS

*SD=System Dependent, *CD=Compiler Dependent, *GV=Garbage Value, *NA=Not Applicable, *NS=Not Specified, *ED=Empty Data Type(for returning nothing), *PT=Pointer Type, *NT=Nothing

2.2 DATA TYPE EXAMPLES

Example in C++	Example in Java	Example in PHP

``cpp
#include <iostream>
int main()
{
char ch='c';
int i=10;
float f=100.1234;
double d=1234.123456;
cout<<"Char="<< ch<<endl;
cout<<"Int="<< i <<endl;
cout<<"Float="<< f<<endl;
cout<<"Double="<<d<<endl;
return 0;
}
Output:
Char=c
Int=10
Float=100.123
Double=1234.12
``
	``java
	public class DataType{
	public static void
	 main(String []args){
	char ch='c';
	System.out.println
	("Char="+ch);
	int i=10;
	System.out.println
	("Int="+i);
	float f=10.1234f;
	System.out.println
	("Float="+f);
	double d=1234.123456;
	System.out.println
	("Double="+d);
	 }
	}
	Output:
	Char=c
	Int=10
	Float=10.1234
	Double=1234.123456
	``
		``php
		<?php
		$x = 'c';
		echo "Char=$x \n";
		$y = 10;
		echo "Int=$y \n";
		$z = 10.1234;
		echo "Float=$z \n";
		$a = 1234.123456;
		echo "Double=$a \n";
		?>
		Output:
		Char=c
		Int=10
		Float=10.1234
		Double=1234.123456
		``

Chapter 3

Operators and Expressions

Operators are used to perform operations on data.

Boolean operator: These operators are usually used on boolean values. *Arithmetic Operator:* These operators are used for numerical operations that takes two operands and performs a calculation on them. *Logical operator:* Compares boolean expressions of two operands and return a boolean result. *Relational operator:* Compares two operands and determine the validity of a relationship. *Assignment operator:* This is used to assign a new value to a variable, object etc. *Operator precedence:* It is predefined rules for specifying the order in which the operators in an expression are evaluated especially when the expression has several operators. *Bitwise operation:* This is used to change individual bits in an operand or operates on one or more bit patterns or binary numerals at the level of their individual bits.

3.1 ARITHMETIC OPERATORS

Operator	Operation	C++	Java	PHP
+	addition	Yes	Yes,String concatenation	Yes
-	subtraction	Yes	Yes	Yes,Negation
*	multiplication	Yes	Yes	Yes
/	division	Yes	Yes	Yes
%	modulo/remainder	Yes	Yes	Yes

3.2 LOGICAL OPERATORS

Name	C++	Java	PHP
logical AND	&&	&&	&& /And
logical OR	||	||	|| Or
logical Not	~	!	!

3.3   BITWISE OPERATORS

Name	C++	Java	PHP
boolean logical AND	&	&	&
boolean logical OR	|	|	|
boolean logical exclusive OR	^	^	^
Shift left	<<	<<	<<
Shift right	>>	>>	>>
Shift right with zero fill	Not Applicable	>>>	Not Applicable

3.4   RELATIONAL/COMPARISON OPERATORS

Operator	Result	C++	Java	PHP
==	Equal to	Yes	Yes	Yes
!=	Not equal to	Yes	Yes	Yes
<	Less than	Yes	Yes	Yes
>	Greater than	Yes	Yes	Yes
<=	Less than or equal to	Yes	Yes	Yes
>=	Greater than or equal to	Yes	Yes	Yes

3.5   ASSIGNMENT OPERATORS

Operator	Description	C++	Java	PHP
=	Simple assignment	Yes	Yes	Yes
+ =	Add AND assignment	Yes	Yes	Yes
− =	Subtract AND assignment	Yes	Yes	Yes
* =	Multiply AND assignment	Yes	Yes	Yes
/ =	Divide AND assignment	Yes	Yes	Yes
% =	Modulus AND assignment	Yes	Yes	Yes
<<=	Left shift AND assignment	Yes	Yes	Yes

>>=	Right shift AND assignment	Yes	Yes	Yes
& =	Bitwise AND assignment	Yes	Yes	Yes
∧=	Bitwise exclusive OR and assignment	Yes	Yes	Yes
| =	Bitwise inclusive OR and assignment	Yes	Yes	Yes

3.6 PRECEDENCE OF OPERATORS

Operator	Description	Associativity in C++	Associativity in Java	Associativity in PHP
::	Scope resolution	Left to right	NA	NA
++, −−	Suffix/postfix increment and decrement	Left to right	Left to right	none
()	Function call	Left to right	Left to right	Left to right
[]	Array subscripting	Left to right	Left to right	Left to right
.	Element selection by reference	Left to right	Left to right	Left to right
− >	Element selection through pointer	Left to right	NA	NA
++, −−	Prefix increment and decrement	Right to left	Right to left	Right to left
+, -	Unary plus and minus	Right to left	Right to left	Right to left
!	Logical NOT	Right to left	Right to left	Right to left
~	bitwise NOT	Right to left	Right to left	none
(type)	Type cast	Right to left	Right to left	Right to left
*	Indirection (dereference)	Right to left	NA	NA
&	Address-of	Right to left	NA	NA
sizeof	Size-of	Right to left	NA	Right to left
new, new[]	Object creation or Dynamic memory allocation	Right to left	Right to left	Right to left
delete, delete[]	Dynamic memory deallocation	Right to left	NA	NA
.*, − > *	Pointer to member	Left to right	NA	NA
*, /, %	Multiplication, division, and remainder	Left to right	Left to right	Left to right
+, -	Addition and subtraction	Left to right	Left to right	Left to right

<<, >>	Bitwise left shift and right shift	Left to right	Left to right	Left to right
<<<	Shift right with zero fill	NA	Left to right	NA
instanceof	instanceof	NA	Left to right	none
clone new	cloning	NA	NA	none
<, <=	For relational operators *Less than* and *Less than or equal to* respectively	Left to right	Left to right	Left to right
>, >=	For relational operators *Greater than* and *Greater than or equal to* respectively	Left to right	Left to right	Left to right
==, !=	For relational *Equal to* and *Not equal to* respectively	Left to right	Left to right	Left to right
&	Bitwise AND	Left to right	Left to right	Left to right
∧	Bitwise XOR (exclusive or)	Left to right	Left to right	Left to right
|	Bitwise OR (inclusive or)	Left to right	Left to right	Left to right
&&	Logical AND	Left to right	Left to right	Left to right
||	Logical OR	Left to right	Left to right	Left to right
?:	Ternary conditional	Right to left	Right to left	Right to left
=	Direct assignment (provided by default for C++ classes)	Right to left	Right to left	Right to left
+=, -=	Assignment by sum and difference	Right to left	Right to left	Right to left
* =, / =, % =	Assignment by product, quotient, and remainder	Right to left	Right to left	Right to left
<<=, >>=	Assignment by bitwise left shift and right shift	Right to left	Right to left	Right to left
&=, ∧=, | =	Assignment by bitwise AND, XOR, and OR	Right to left	Right to left	Right to left
throw	Throw operator (for exceptions)	Right to left	Right to left	Right to left
,	comma	Left to right	Left to right	Left to right

*NA= Not Applicable

3.7   EVALUATION OF LOGICAL OPERATIONS (SAME FOR C++/JAVA/PHP)

Operator	Description	Evaluation Description	Example(A=1,B=0)
&&	AND operator	If both the operands are non zero then condition becomes true	(A && B) is false
||	OR Operator	If any of the two operands is non zero then condition becomes true	(A ||B) is true
!	NOT Operator	Use to reverses the logical state of its operand. If a condition is true then Logical NOT operator will make false	!(A && B) is true

3.8   EVALUATION OF BITWISE/BINARY OPERATIONS (SAME FOR C++/JAVA/PHP)

Operator	Description	Evaluation Description	Example(A=3,B=5)
&	AND Operator	copies a bit to the result if it exists in both operands	(A & B) will give 1 which is 0001
|	OR Operator	copies a bit if it exists in either operand	(A |B) will give 7 which is 0111
∧	XOR Operator	copies the bit if it is set in one operand but not both	(A ∧ B) will give 6 which is 0110
~	Ones Complement Operator	It is a unary and has the effect of 'flipping' bits	(~A) will give -3 which is 1111111111111100 for 16 bit integers
<<	Left Shift Operator	The left operands value is moved left by the number of bits specified by the right operand	A << 2 will give 12 which is 1100
>>	Right Shift Operator	The left operands value is moved right by the number of bits specified by the right operand	A >> 2 will give 0 which is 0000

Chapter 4

Control Flow Statements

Branching statement is used to change the control flow in the program.

4.1 DECISION MAKING STATEMENTS

Statement	Description	Syntax and example in C++	Syntax and example in Java	Syntax and example in PHP

if-then	Executes a a piece of code only if a particular condition/test evaluates to *true*.	Syntax:
		`if( condition )`
		`{`
		`  statements;`
		`}`
		Example:
		`int x=0;`
		`if ( x > 0 )`
		`{`
		`  cout << "Hi";`
		`}`
			Syntax:
			`if( condition )`
			`{`
			`  statements;`
			`}`
			Example:
			`int x=0;`
			`if ( x > 0 )`
			`{`
			`System.out.`
			`println("Hi");`
			`}`
				Syntax:
				`if( condition )`
				`{`
				`  statements;`
				`}`
				Example:
				`$x = 0;`
				`if ($x > 0)`
				`{`
				`    echo 'Hi';`
				`}`

| if-then-else | Executes a piece of code when an "if" clause evaluates to *false* , else-if can be added as many branched conditions as possible. | Syntax:
`if( condition )`
`{`
`  statements;`
`}`
`else`
`{`
`  statements;`
`}`
Example:
`int x=0;`
`if ( x > 0 )`
`{`
`  cout << "Hi";`
`}`
`else`
`{`
`  cout << "Hello";`
`}` | Syntax:
`if( condition )`
`{`
`  statements;`
`}`
`else`
`{`
`  statements;`
`}`
Example:
`int x=0;`
`if ( x > 0 )`
`{`
`System.out.`
`println("Hi");`
`}`
`else`
`{`
`System.out.`
`println("Hello");`
`}` | Syntax:
`if( condition )`
`{`
`  statements;`
`}`
`else`
`{`
`  statements;`
`}`
Example:
`$x = 0;`
`if ($x > 0)`
`{`
`    echo 'Hi';`
`}`
`else`
`{`
`    echo 'Hello';`
`}` |

switch	This statement gives number of possible execution paths, statements under a case will be executed if expression is equal to case value.	Syntax:
		`switch(expression)`
		`{`
		`  case cs1:`
		`    statements`
		`    break;`
		`. . .`
		`    case csN:`
		`      statements`
		`      break;`
		`. . .`
		`    default:`
		`      statements`
		`}`
		Example:
		`char x='a';`
		`switch (x)`
		`{`
		`  case 'a':`
		`    cout << "Hi";`
		`    break;`
		`  case 'b':`
		`    cout << "Hello";`
		`    break;`
		`  default:`
		`    cout << "Bye";`
		`    break;`
		`}`
			Syntax:
			`switch(expression)`
			`{`
			`  case cs1:`
			`    statements`
			`    break;`
			`. . .`
			`    case csN:`
			`      statements`
			`      break;`
			`. . .`
			`    default:`
			`      statements`
			`}`
			Example:
			`char x='a';`
			`switch (x)`
			`{`
			`  case 'a':`
			`    System.out.`
			`    println("Hi");`
			`    break;`
			`  case 'b':`
			`    System.out.`
			`    println("Hello");`
			`    break;`
			`  default:`
			`    System.out.`
			`    println("Bye");`
			`    break;`
			`}`
				Syntax:
				`switch(expression)`
				`{`
				`  case cs1:`
				`    statements`
				`    break;`
				`. . .`
				`  case csN:`
				`    statements`
				`    break;`
				`. . .`
				`  default:`
				`    statements`
				`}`
				Example:
				`$x='a';`
				`switch ($x)`
				`{`
				`  case 'a':`
				`    echo 'Hi';`
				`    break;`
				`  case 'b':`
				`    echo 'Hello';`
				`    break;`
				`  default:`
				`    echo 'Bye';`
				`    break;`
				`}`

| declare | This statement gives number of possible execution paths. | Not Applicable | Not Applicable | ```
Syntax:
declare(directive)
statement
Example:
1).
declare(encoding=
'ISO-8859-1');
//your script

2).
declare(ticks=1) {
//your script
}
``` |
|---|---|---|---|---|

4.2 LOOPING STATEMENTS

Statement	Description	Syntax and example in C++	Syntax and example in Java	Syntax and example in PHP
| for | This statement provides a compact way to iterate over a range of specified values. A *for* loop should have a initialization(init), a condition(cond) expression to terminate the loop and the last invocation statement is increment(incr) or decrement(decr) expression and it will be invoked after each iteration through the loop. | ```
Syntax:
for(init;cond;incr)
{
    statements;
}
Example:
for( int i = 0;
i < 5; i++ )
{
    cout << i;
}
``` | ```
Syntax:
for(init;cond;incr)
{
    statements;
}
Example:
for ( int i = 0;
i < 5; i++ )
{
 System.out.
 println(i);
}
``` | ```
Syntax:
for(init;cond;incr)
{
    statements;
}
Example:
for ( $i = 0;
$i < 5; $i++ )
{
 echo $i;
}
``` |

for-each	Iteration over arrays and other collections.	NA (It is supported in Visual C++)	Syntax:
			for(type item:
			iterableCollection)
			{
			// do something
			// to item
			}
			Example:
			int[] arr = {1, 2};
			for(double d : arr)
			{
			  System.out.
			  println(d);
			}
				Syntax:
				foreach($set as
				$val)
				{
				// do something
				//to $val;
				}
				Example:
				<?php
				$arr = array(1, 2);
				foreach($arr as $d)
				{
				  echo "$d";
				}
				?>

while	This statement continually executes a block of code while a particular condition is *true*.	Syntax:
		while(expression)
		{
		statement(s);
		}
		Example:
		int x = 0;
		while (x < 5)
		{
		cout<<x++;
		}
			Syntax:
			while(expression)
			{
			statement(s);
			}
			Example:
			int x = 0;
			while (x < 5)
			{
			System.out.
			println(x++);
			}
				Syntax:
				while(expression)
				{
				statement(s);
				}
				Example:
				$x = 0;
				while ($x < 5)
				{
				echo $x++;
				}

do-while	This statement evaluates expression at the bottom of the loop instead of the top.	Syntax:
		do{
		  statement(s);
		}while(condition);
		
		Example:
		int x = 0;
		do
		{
		cout<<x++;
		} while (x < 5);
			Syntax:
			do{
			  statement(s);
			}while(condition);
			
			Example:
			int x = 0;
			do
			{
			System.out.
			println(x++);
			} while (x < 5);
				Syntax:
				do{
				  statement(s);
				}while(condition);
				
				Example:
				$x = 0;
				do
				{
				echo $x++;
				}while ($x < 5);

4.3   BRANCHING STATEMENTS

Statement	Description	Syntax and example in C++	Syntax and example in Java	Syntax and example in PHP

break	End a loop. *break* causes an immediate exit from the switch and exit from *while* or *do-while* or *for* loop.	Syntax:
		break;
		
		Example:
		int x = 0;
		do
		{
		  if (x == 3)
		  break;
		  x++;
		}while (x < 5);
			1)Labelled Syntax:
			break;
			2)Unlabelled
			Syntax:
			break label;
			Example:
			1)
			int x = 0;
			do
			{
			  if (x == 3)
			  break;
			  x++;
			}while (x < 5);
			2)
			1)int x = 0;
			jump:
			do
			{
			  if (x == 3)
			  break jump;
			  x++;
			}while (x < 5);
				1)Labelled Syntax:
				break;
				2)Unlabelled
				Syntax:
				break label;
				
				Example:
				1)
				$x = 0;
				do
				{
				  if ($x == 3)
				  break;
				  $x++;
				}while ($x< 5);
				2)
				$x = 0;
				do
				{
				  if ($x == 3)
				  break lbl;
				  $x++;
				  lbl:
				  echo "Jumped !";
				}while ($x< 5);

| continue | Control inside a loop can be continued even when the specified loop condition is not true and this statement applies only to loops(for, while, or do-while loop), not to switch. | Syntax:
continue;

Example:
int x = 0;
while (x < 5)
{
  if(x == 3)
      continue;
cout<<x++;
} | 1)Labelled Syntax:
continue;
2)Unlabelled
Syntax:
continue label;

Example:
1)
int x = 0;
while (x < 5)
{
  if(x == 3)
      continue;
System.out.
println(x++);
}
2)
int x = 0;
lbl:
while (x < 5)
{
  if(x == 3)
      continue lbl;
System.out.
println(x++);
} | Syntax:
  continue;

Example:
$x = 0;
while ($x < 5)
{
if(x == 3)
      continue;
echo $x++;
} |
| goto | This can be used to jump to another section in the program. | Syntax:
goto label;
statement(s);
label: statement;

Example:
int x = 0;
lbl:
while (x < 5)
{
  if(x == 3)
      goto lbl;
cout<<x++;
} | NA | Syntax:
goto label;
statement(s);
label: statement;

Example:
goto b;
  echo 'Hi';
  b:
  echo 'Hello'; |

return	Explicitly return from a method. Control flow returns to where the method was invoked.	1)return with value
		Syntax: return;
		2)return without value
		Syntax: return expression;
		
		Example:
		1)
		void method()
		{
		//statement(s);
		return;
		}
		2)
		boolean method()
		{
		//statement(s);
		return false;
		}
			1)return with value
			Syntax: return;
			2)return without value
			Syntax: return expression;
			
			Example:
			1)
			void method()
			{
			//statement(s);
			return;
			}
			2)
			boolean method()
			{
			//statement(s);
			return false;
			}
				1)return with value
				Syntax: return;
				2)return without value
				Syntax: return expression;
				
				Example:
				1)
				function fun()
				{
				    return;
				}
				2)
				function add($x)
				{
				    $dbl=$x+$x;
				    return $dbl;
				}

exit	Terminates the running process.	Syntax:
		exit(value):
		
		Example:
		int x=0;
		if (x < 0)
		    exit(1);
			Syntax:
			System.exit(val);
			
			Example:
			int x=0;
			if(x == null)
			{
			  System.exit(1);
			}
				Syntax:
				exit;
				exit();
				exit(value);
				
				Example:
				//exit program
				//normally
				exit;
				exit();
				exit(0);
				
				//exit with an
				//error code
				exit(1);
				exit(0376);//octal

die	Equivalent to exit.	NA	NA	

				Syntax:
				die();
				die(message)
				
				Example:
				$site = "http://www.google.com/";
				fopen($site,"r")
				or die("$site is down !");

*NA=Not Applicable

4.4 EXCEPTION HANDLING

Enclosing the code within a try block that might throw an exception. *try-catch-throw* is supported in C++ and PHP and *try-catch-throw-finally* is supported in JAVA. Syntax of exception handling is given in following table,

Syntax and example in C++	Syntax and example in Java	Syntax and example in PHP

Syntax:
1)try {statements} catch (exception-decl) {statem ents}
2)try {statements} catch (exception-decl_1...exc-eption-decl_n{statements}
3)try {statements} catch (exception-decl){stateme nts throw; }
4)try { statements } cat ch (exception-decl-1){st atements} catch(exceptio n-decl-2) {statements }
 	
Example:
try
{
int* arr= new int[1000];
}
catch (exception& e)
{
 cout << "Exception: "
    << e.what() << endl;
}
	Syntax:
	try {
	//code
	} catch(ExceptionType name){
	//code
	} catch(ExceptionType name){
	//code
	}
	finally{
	//code
	}
	
	Example:
	BufferedReader buff ;
	try {
	buff= new BufferedReader(new FileReader("C:\\testing.txt"));
	buff.readLine();
	}catch(Exception exe)
	{
	   exe.printStackTrace();
	}
	finally {
	System.out.println("Finally
	    Executed");
	}
		Syntax:
		try
		{
		 // code
		}
		catch (exception-decl)
		{
		throw new Exception (parameters);
		}
		
		Example:
		try
		{
		if(filter_var($email, FILTER_VALIDATE_EMAIL) === FALSE)
		{
		 throw new customException ($email);
		}
		}
		
		catch (customException $e)
		{
		//display custom message
		echo $e->errorMessage();
		}

Chapter 5

Arrays

An array is a well arranged set of objects or values, usually in rows and columns.

5.1 ARRAYS

Description	C++	Java	PHP
Definition	An array is a sequence of elements of the same type located in contiguous memory locations that can be individually referenced by adding an index to a distinctive identifier.	Similar to C++. An array is a storage place object that holds a rigid number of values of a single type.	An array is association of values and keys in ordered map. The values in array can be other arrays, trees and multi-dimensional arrays are also possible.
Syntax of 1D Array	type name [elements];	type arrayName = new type[size];	Index Array: $arrayName = array(value1, value2, value3, etc.); Associativity Array: $arrayName = array(key1⇒ value1, key2⇒ value2, key3⇒ value3, etc.);
Syntax of 2D Array	type name [rows][cols];	type arrayName = new type[rows][cols];	$arrayName = array(array(value1, value2, value3, etc.));

Example of 1D Array(one of the ways)	int arr[10]; // *arr* is an array of length 10 arr[0] =14; // set the 1st element of array *arr*	int [] arr; // *arr* is an array arr = new int [10]; // now *arr* points to an array of length 10 arr[0] = 14; // set the 1st element of the array pointed to by *arr*	
Default value	Garbage Value	A initial value is assigned to each element of a newly allocated array if no initial value is specified. The default value is depends upon the type of the array elements used, e.g, default value for *boolean* has *false* , similarly *char* has '0̌000', *byte or int or short or int or long or float or double* has *0* and any pointer has *null* value	There is no default value except *SplFixedArray*. For *SplFixedArray*, default value is NULL.
Accessing out of array size	Undefined Behaviour	This causes a Runtime Exception like array Out Of Bond Exception in case of using *SplFixedArray*	This causes Runtime Exception like 'Index invalid or out of range.

Find Array Length	Total length of array is calculated by *total size of array / size of array data type*, e.g, int arr[]={1,2,3,4}; int size = sizeof(arr) / sizeof(int); // length is 4	int [] arr = new int[10]; int arrLength = arr.length; // length is 10	*count(array,mode)* counts the number of elements of an array or the properties of an object with array/object name and optional mode like 0(default value to not consider Multi Dimensional Array)/1(considering Multi Dimensional Array), e.g, <?php $arr = array(1, 2, 3); echo count($arr); ?>

Array passing to function	Option 1) Formal parameters as an un-sized array int getSum(int arr[], int size) { int i, sum = 0; for (i = 0; i < size; ++i) { sum += arr[i]; } return sum; } # include <iostream> using namespace std; int getSum(int arr[]); int main () { int a[5] = 1, 2, 3, 4, 5; cout << "Sum: " << getSum(a, 5); return 0; } Option 2: Formal parameters as a pointer #include¡iostream¿ using namespace std; int sum(int *arr, int size); int sum(int *arr, int size) int sum = 0; for (int i = 0; i ¡ size; i++) sum += arr[i]; return sum; int main() int a[] = 1,2,3,4,5 ; cout¡¡sum(a, 5); return 0; Option 3: Formal parameters as a sized array #include¡iostream¿ using namespace std; int sum(int arr[5]); int sum(int arr[5]) int sum = 0; for (int i = 0; i ¡= sizeof(arr); i++) sum += arr[i]; return sum; int main() int a[] = 1,2,3,4,5 ; cout¡¡sum(a); return 0;	Option 1: Passing local array class Main public static void main (String[] args) int arr1[]=1,2,3,4,5; int[] arr2=6,7,8,9,10; int add=sum(arr1,arr2); System.out.println(add); public static int sum(int a1[], int a2[]) return a1[1]+a2[4]; Option-2:Create an array on the fly and pass it class Main public static void main (String[] args) int add=sum(new int[] 1,2,3,4,5, new int[] 6,7,8,9,10); System.out.println(add); public static int sum(int a1[], int a2[]) return a1[1]+a2[4];	Option 1: Passing arguments by default Option 2: Passing by reference Option 3: Default argument values. Variable-length argument lists are also supported, see also the function references for $func_numargs()$, $func_getarg()$, and $func_getargs()$for more information.

Chapter 6

Strings

String is a sequence(ordered) of characters.

6.1 STRINGS

Few APIs/Methods for Strings are self explanatory. PHP has no specific command for declaring a string variable as it is a Loosely Typed Language. A variable is created the moment you first assign a value to it.

Features	C++	Java	PHP
Declaration	string str;	String str1 ;	str1="Hello world!"; $str2=(string) NULL;
Initialization	string str1("hi"); string str2 = "Hello" string str3("Hi"); string str4(10, 'h'); string str5=str3;	String str1="hi"; String str2= new String("hello"); String str3= str1; String str4= null;	str1="Hello world!"; $str2=(string) NULL; $str3=(string) 1234;

Concatenation	str1 += str2;
	str = str1 + str2;
	str = str1 + "Hi";
	str = "Hello"+"Hi";
		String str1="hi";
		String str2= new
		String("hello");
		String str3= str1
		+str2+"fine"+1;
		String str4=
		str1.concat(str2);
		StringBuilder and
		StringBuffer can
		be used for enha
		-nced String
		operations.
			$str1="ABCD";
			$str2=
			(string)"ABCD";
			$str3=
			$str1."A".$str2;

Accessing a char
or index of char
	str[index];
	str.at(index);
	str(index, count);
		String str1="ABCD";
		str1.charAt(2);
		str1.indexOf('B');
		str1.
		lastIndexOf('B');
		int fromIndex=2;
		str1.indexOf('B',
		fromIndex);
		str1.lastIndexOf
		('B',fromIndex);
			$st="ABCD";
			echo $st{2};
			echo $st[2];
			echo strrpos
			($st,"C");

Accessing sub
-string or
index of
substring
	string
	str="abcdefgh";
	cout <<
	str.substr(1,6);
	cout <<
	str.find("abc");
		String str1=
		"ABCDEF";
		String str2="ABCDE";
		str1.substring(5,8);
		str1.substring(5);
		str1.indexOf(str2);
		str1.
		lastIndexOf(str2);
			strpos(), stripos(),
			strripos(),substr(),
			strstr() etc.

Comparison	if (str1 < str2) cout <<"Hi"; if (str1 == str2) cout <<"Hi"; if (str1 > str2) cout <<"Hi";	Methods to compare strings, endsWith(), startsWith(), compareTo(), compareTo-IgnoreCase(), equals(), equalsIgnoreCase(), regionMatches(), regionMatches(), matches() etc.	strcmp(), strcasecmp(), preg_match(), substr_compare(), strncmp() etc
String Length	str.length();	String str1 = "ABCDEF"; str1.length(); "ABCDEF".length();	$str = 'ABCDEF'; echo strlen($str);
Output a string	cout<<str; cout<< setw(width)<<str;	String st = "ABCDEF"; System.out. println(st);	echo $str;

Chapter 7

Functions

A function(method) is a group of statements or block of code that together perform a task which can be called from any point in a code after it has been declared.

7.1 FUNCTIONS

Functions have autonomous existence means they are defined outside of the class e.g. main() in C++ is a function. Whereas methods do not have independent existence they are all the time defined inside class e.g. main() in JAVA is called method. A method in PHP is tied to a specific class. **Parts of a function:**

Return Type (ret_type): A method/function may return a value (void if no value ruturns). The ret_type is the data type of the value the function returns(ret_type is not required in PHP).

Function Name (fun_name): This is a name of function.

Parameters (param_list or param_val): It is a optional list. Value/object passing as parameter. This value/object is referred to as actual parameter or argument by referring its type, order, and number of the parameters of a function.

Body of Function: The function body contains a collection of statements which serve the purpose of a logic.

Modifier Name(modifier_name): This is called as visibility(access type) of a method that instructs the compiler how to call/access a method. In some cases this is optional.

Calling a Function: To execute a method or function, it is required to pass the necessary parameters along with function name and if function returns a value then you can store returned value then program control is transferred to the called function. A called function performs defined job and when its return statement is executed or when it reached end of function with closing brace, it returns program control back to the calling or main program.

Parameter Order Association: Required to provide arguments in the same order as their respective parameters in the method design.

Features	C++	Java	PHP
| Syntax | ```
modifier_name:
ret_type fun_name
(param_list)
{
//body of the function
}
``` | ```
modifier_name ret_type
fun_name(param_list) {
//body of the function
}
``` | ```
modifier_name function
fun_name(param_list){
//body of the function
}
``` |
| Example | ```
#include<iostream>
class Test
{
 public:
void method1(int);
void method2(int x)
     {
   cout << "x="<<x;
     }
};
void Test::
method1(int y)
{
cout << "y="<<y;
}
int main()
{
   Test t;
   t.method1(10);
   t.method2(20);
   return 0;
}
``` | ```
class Test {
public static void
main(String[] args){
  Test t= new Test();
  t.method(10);
}
public void
method(int x)
{
System.out.println(x);
}
}
``` | ```
<?php
function method()
{
echo "Hi";
}
method();
?>
``` |
| Declarations | It tells to compiler about a function name and how to make a call to function.

Syntax:
```
ret_type fun_name
(param_list);
```
Example:
```
int method(int arg1,
int arg2);
``` | Needs to provide access keyword in addition to C++ syntax.

Syntax:
```
modifier_name ret_type
fun_name(param_list);
```
Example:
```
public int method(int
arg1, int arg2);
``` | PHP function can write on top of the document where the function will be used, or in a separate file (use PHP function such as include_once() to access such functions)

```
function fun_name() {
 return 'Hi';
}
``` |
| Calling a Function | Syntax:
```
ret_type var_name
fun_name(param_val);
```
Example:
```
int ret =
 method(10,20);
``` | Syntax:
```
ret_type var_name
fun_name(param_val);
```
Example:
```
int ret = method
(10,20);
``` | Syntax:
```
$var_name = method
(param_val);
```
Example:
```
$ret =
method(10, 20);
``` |

call by value (pass by value) or call by Reference (pass by Reference) or call by Pointer (pass by Pointer)	Supports all three (default:call by value)	call by value(default)	call by reference(&$var), call by value(default)
Defaulting Parameter's Value	```int method(int a, int b=20) { return = a + b; } int main () { int a = 100; cout <<method(a); }```	This is not supported(It can be evaluated through method overloading.).	```<?php function method($num, $num1=111) { $num += $num1; } $val= 10; method(&$val); echo "$val"; ?>```
Indefinite Parameters in function	```#include<iostream.h> void method(int Num, ...) { va_list Numlist; va_start(Numlist, Num); int add = 0; for(int i = 0; i < Num; ++i) { add += va_arg(Numlist, int); } va_end(Numlist); cout<<(add/Num); } int main() { method(3, 0, 1,2); return 0; }```	```class Test{ public static void main(String[] args) { method('A','B','C'); } public static void method(char...charr){ for(char a: charr) System.out.println(a); } }```	```<?php function method(){ foreach(func_get_args() as $a) { echo $a; } } echo method('A','B','C', 'D','E','F'); ?>```

Method Overloading and Method Overriding	Yes. Overriding Example:	Yes. Overriding Example:	Yes. Overriding Example:

	``cpp
	#include <iostream>
	using namespace std;
	class A {
	public:
	virtual void M(){
	cout<<"A";
	}
	};
	class B : public A {
	public:
	void M() {
	cout<<"B";
	}
	};
	
	int main()
	{
	B a;
	a.M();
	A b;
	A *c = &b;
	c->M();
	return 0;
	}
	``
	Overloading Example:
	``cpp
	#include <iostream>
	class T {
	public:
	void M(int i, int j)
	{
	cout<<"A="<<i+j;
	}
	
	void M(int i,double j)
	{
	cout<<"A="<<i+j;
	}
	void M(double i,
	double j)
	{
	cout<<"A="<<i+j;
	}
	};
	int main(){
	T t;
	t.M(1,1);
	t.M(1,1.1);
	t.M(1.1,1.1);
	return 0;
	}
	``
		``java
		class A{
		public void M(){
		System.out.
		println("A");
		}
		}
		class B extends A{
		public void M(){
		System.out
		.println("B");
		}
		}
		public class Test{
		public static void
		main(String args[]){
		A a = new A();
		A b = new B();
		a.M();
		b.M();
		    }
		}
		``
		
		Overloading Example:
		``java
		class T {
		public void M(int i,
		 int j)
		{
		System.out.println
		("A="+ (i+j));
		}
		
		public void M(int i,
		 double j)
		{
		System.out.println
		("B="+ (i+j));
		}
		public static void
		main(String str[]){
		T t = new T();
		t.M(1,1);
		t.M(1,1.1);
		}
		}
		``
			``php
			<?php
			class A {
			public function m($p)
			{
			echo "$p";
			}
			}
			class B extends A {
			public function m($p)
			{
			echo "$p";
			}
			}
			$a = new A;
			$b = new B;
			$a->m('A');
			$b->m('B');
			?>
			``
			
			Overloading Example:
			``php
			<?php
			class T
			{
			public function __call
			($method_name , $param)
			{
			if($method_name == "M")
			{
			$count = count($param);
			switch($count)
			{
			case "1":
			echo "1";
			break;
			case "2":
			echo "2";
			break;
			default:
			echo "0";
			}
			}
			}
			}
			$a = new T();
			$a->M();
			$a->M("1");
			$a->M("1" , "2");
			?>
			``

Chapter 8

Classes

A class is the template or blueprint from which objects are created.

8.1 CLASSES

Features	C++	Java	PHP
Syntax	```class class_name{ visibility_type: Variables declarations; Methods definitions; }; int main() { //call methods //via instances }```	```class class_name{ Variables declarations; Methods definitions; public static void main(String args[]){ { //call methods //via instances } }```	PHP's entry point is defined as the first line in the first file that gets executed. ```<?php class class_name{ Variables declarations; Methods definitions; } //call methods //via instances ?>```
Example	```class A{ public: int a; A(): a(2) {} int M(){ return a+a; } }; int main() { A a; cout<<a.M(); return 0; }```	```class A { int M(int b){ return b+b; } public static void main(String args[]){ A a= new A(); System.out.println (a.M(2)); } }```	```<?php class A { public $a= 'Hello'; public function M() { echo $this->a; } } $a = new A(); $a->M(); ?>```

39

Parts of Class	data items (members) and functions (member functions)	data items (members) and functions (member functions)	data items (members) and functions (member functions)
Overloading	Supports functions and operators overloading.	Supports functions overloading.	Supports functions and operators overloading.
Inheritance (Single, Multiple, Multilevel, Hierarchical and Hybrid)	Supports all types.	Supports Single level, hierarchical level and Multilevel. Multiple Inheritance directly not supported like C++, but it can be achieved through *interface*.	Supports Single level, hierarchical level and Multilevel. Multiple inheritance not supported directly but can be achieved through use of *interface*.
Data Abstraction and Encapsulation	Supports.	Supports.	Supports.
Polymorphism	Supports.	Supports.	Supports.

Chapter 9

Objects

Object is an instance of a Class which has states (fields) and behaviours (methods).

9.1 OBJECTS

Object creation may include below steps,
Declaration: A variable name with an object type.
Instantiation: Most popular *new* keyword is used to create the object.
Initialization: The *new* keyword is followed by a call to a constructor will initialize the new object.

Features	C++	Java	PHP
Syntax (Creating Object)	1)*class_name object_name = new class_name;/*constructors* value can be passed */ They create the objects in different parts of the memory (heap vs stack) with object lifetime. The code manages the memory allocation explicitly, and it must also manage the deallocation explicitly (using delete/delete[]) 2)*class_name object_name;* The object and its space is automatically deallocated at the end of its enclosing scope (either a method, a nested block within a method, or a class) 3)*class_name* object_name = (class_name*) malloc(sizeof (class_name));* Allocating (malloc, calloc and realloc) storage space for the object.	1)*class_name1 object_name = new class_name2;* The *new* keyword is used to create an object in Java. 2)*class_name1 object_name = (class_name2) Class.forName("class_name3"). newInstance();* If we know the name of the class(class_name3) and if it has a public default constructor we can create an object in this way. 3)*class_name1 obj = new class_name2();* *class_name3 xyz = obj.clone();* Objects can be created by copying of an existing object. 4) *ObjectInputStream inStream = new ObjectInput- Stream(anInputStream);* *Class_Name object_name = (Class_Name) inStream.readObject();* Object deserialization is nothing but creating an object from its serialized form. 5)*class_name1 object_name=this.getClass(). getClass- Loader().loadClass(class_name2).newInstance();* Create object using class loader.	1)*$object_name = new class_name;* The *new* keyword is used to create an object in PHP. 2)*$object_name = new class_name(constructor param type with functions);* PHP Anonymous Object

Example	i)A *a = new A;
	ii)A a; or A a(param1);
	iii) Obj* obj = (Obj*) malloc(sizeof(Obj));
		i)Class_Name object = new Class_Name();
		ii)Class_Name object = (Class_Name) Class.forName ("subin.rnd.abc"). newInstance();
		iii) Class_Name anotherObject = new Class_Name();
		Class_Name object = anotherObject.clone();
		iv) ObjectInputStream inStream = new ObjectInput-Stream(anInputStream);
		Class_Name object = (Class_Name) inStream.readObject();
		v)Class_Name object this.getClass(). getClass-Loader().loadClass(com.abc.Test).newInstance();
			i)$phpbook = new Books;
			ii)$object_name = new class_name(array("hi" ⇒ function() echo "hi";));
			or $obj = (object) array('hi' ⇒ 'hi1', 'hello' ⇒ 'hello1');

Deallocating the memory(Releasing Unused Objects)	*delete object or delete[] object* operation is used to de-allocate the memory which is dynamically allocated using *new* operation.
	Example:
	`delete obj;`
	`delete[] obj;`
		JVM will deallocate the object when an object is no longer referenced. The garbage collector(*System.gc()*) works automatically in the background, the *super.finalize()*; method is run only if the garbage collector attempts to reclaim the object. Example:
		
		`protected void`
		`finalize() throws`
		`Throwable`
		`{`
		`super.finalize();`
		`}`
			The destructor (*__destruct*) method will be called as soon as there are no other references to a particular object(implicitly), or in any order during the shutdown sequence. Example:
			
			`public function`
			`__destruct()`
			`{`
			`//code`
			`}`
			
			The *unset()* function destroys a given object or variable.
			
			Syntax:
			`void unset`
			`(VarOrObject...)`
			Example:
			`$test='hi';`
			`unset($test);`

Accessing Class fields and methods bypassing Object Creation. Static data members and static functions are accessed directly via class name itself without using an object of class.	Syntax:
	1)data_type
	 class_name
	:: field_name();
	2)ret_type
	class_name
	:: method_name();
	Example:
	1)static int i;
	\\defined within
	\\class A
	int A::i = 1;
	\\ Code outside
	\\class A
	2)static int
	 method(){}
	\\defined within
	\\ class A
	int A::method();
	\\ Code outside
	\\ class A
		Syntax:
		class_name.
		field_name;
		class_name.
		method_name();
		Example:
		1)static int i;
		//define in class A
		A.i=1;
		//Code outside
		//class A
		2)static void
		method(){}
		//define in class A
		A.method();
		//Code outside
		//class A
			Syntax:
			class_name::field;
			class_name::method();
			Example:
			1)static $a;
			//define in class A
			A::$a = array();
			//Code outside class A
			2)public static
			function method(){}
			//define in class A
			A::method();
			//Code outside class A
			3)$classname = 'A';
			$classname::method();

Chapter 10

Inheritance

Inheritance is the process where code and functionality can be reused by acquiring the properties of another class.

10.1   INHERITANCE

Inheritance reduces the implementation time, easy code management and helps hierarchical information ordering.

Base Class (Super Class): It is the class whose properties are inherited by another class (e.g Sub class).

Derived Class (Sub Class): It is the class that inherit properties from base class(es).

Single Inheritance: One derived class inherits properties from one base class.

Multiple Inheritance: One derived class inherits from multiple base class(es).

Hierarchical Inheritance: Multiple subclasses inherit from one base class.

Multilevel Inheritance: Subclass acts as a base class for other classes.

Hybrid Inheritance: It is the valid combination of Single/ Multiple/ Hierarchical/ Multilevel.

Class inheritance (extends): Constructs a new class as an extension of another class to reuse the code. That is, the derived class inherits the public methods and public data of the super class. Java only allows a class to have one immediate base class, i.e., single inheritance.

Interface inheritance (implements): Constructs a new class to implement the methods defined as part of an interface for the reason of sub typing. Java supports multiple interface inheritance.

Overloading : Defining functions that have similar signatures with different parameters.

Overriding: This technique works w.r.t Base class(parent) and derived class(sub class), where the base class has defined a method and the derived class wishes to override or bypass that method.

Is-a relationship: This relationship is used for inheritance between a parent class and its Subclass. *extends* and *implements* keywords are used to describe this in Java and PHP.

Example: Vehicle is super class of Car, Car is sub class of Vehicle, then Car IS-A Vehicle.

Features	C++	Java	PHP
Types of Inheritance Supported	Single Inheritance, Multiple Inheritance, Multilevel Inheritance , Hierarchical Inheritance and Hybrid Inheritance.	Support all inheritance(Single, Multilevel, Multiple, Hierarchical, and Hybrid) except Multiple inheritance, but we can achieve multiple inheritance through *interface*.	Support all inheritance(Single, Multilevel, Multiple, Hierarchical, and Hybrid) except Multiple inheritance, but we can achieve multiple inheritance through *interface*.
Class Inheritance or/and Interface Inheritance	Supports Class Inheritance	Supports both.	Supports both.
Overriding and Overloading of method(function)	Supports.	Supports.	Supports.
What is not inheritable from base class?	its constructor and its destructor, its operator=() members and its friends.	Its private members and static methods are not inheritable. Constructors are not inherited by subclasses, but the constructor of the superclass can be invoked from the subclass.	Its private members and static methods are not inheritable.
instanceof operator	Does not have *instanceof* operator. But alternatively we can satisfy the needs by using *dynamic_cast* and templates.	Supports.	Supports.
Accessibility	*public:*Anybody can access. *protected:*The base class can only be accessed by its inherited subclasses. *private:* Nobody can access except itself.	*Public:* Visible to all wherever its class is used. *Private:* Visible to the class only. *protected:* Visible to the package and all its subclasses of any package.	*public:*Class members declared public can be accessed everywhere. *protected:*Members declared protected can be accessed only within the class itself and inherited members. *private:*Members declared as private may only be accessed by the class that defines the member.

Chapter 11

Constructors and Destructors

Constructor: It is a method/function usually used to create the object and/or initialize the objects.
Destructor(C++,PHP):
Destructors are the opposite of constructors in terms of deallocating memory and releasing the object for cleanup purpose when that object goes out of scope or is explicitly deleted.

11.1 CONSTRUCTORS AND DESTRUCTORS

Rules of Constructor/Destructor:
→ Constructor/Destructor cannot be overridden.
→ Constructor can be overloaded.
→ There is only one Destructor per class in C++.
→ A class does not inherit Constructor/Destructor from any of its base class.
→ Constructors are used to initialize the instance variables of an object and Destructor is used to destroy the unreferenced objects.
→ Constructors are similar to methods, during creation of a new instance (a new object) of a class using the new keyword, a constructor for that class is called.
→ Constructor/Destructor do not have return types.
→ The first line of a constructor must either be a call on another constructor in the same class (this), or a call on the superclass constructor (using super).
→ Constructor/Destructor are invoked automatically whenever the object is created.

Features	C++	Java	PHP
Rules of Constructor	Same as above description with following rules, → It has same name of its class. → Constructor cannot be inherited. → Constructor can not be virtual. → Not possible to refers to the address of constructors. → Not possible to use the constructor as member of union if the object is created with constructor. → Constructors cannot be declared static, const, or volatile.	Same as above description. → It has same name of its class. → Constructor cannot be inherited.	Same as above description with following rules, → Starting with PHP 5.3.3. methods with the same name as the last element of a namespaced class name will no longer be treated as constructors. In PHP, _construct is used invoke the constructor. → Constructor can be inherited.

Syntax of Constructor	`NameOfClass::`
	`NameOfClass (optional arguments){}`
		`<optional visibility>`
		`NameOfClass`
		`(optional`
		`arguments){}`
			`function __construct`
			`([mixed`
			`$args[, $... ]] ){}`

Example of Constructor	```class Test
{
public:
Test(int number);
int getNum();
private:
int num;
};
Test::Test(int i)
{
num=i;
}
int Test::getNum()
{
return num;
}

int main(){
Test t(100);
cout<<t.getNum();
return 0;
}``` | ```class Test {
int num;
public Test(int num){
this.num = num;
}
public int getNum(){
return this.num;
}
public static void
main(String str[])
{
Test t= new
Test(100);
System.out.println(
t.getNum());
}
}``` | ```<?php
class Test {
private $num;
public function
__construct() {
$num = "";
}
function __destruct() {
}
public function setNum
($num) {
$this->num = $num;
}
public function getNum()
{
return $this->num;
}
}
$t = new Test();
$t->setNum(100);
echo $t->getNum();
?>``` |

Rules of Destructor	→ The destructor has the same name as the class, but with a tilde ( ) prefixing it. If the object is creating with a *new* expression, then destructor is called when the delete operator is applied to a pointer to the object. → A destructor should never throw an exception.	There is no explicit destructor in Java. Garbage Collection(GC) in JVM does cleanup the heap and destroys unused objects or unreferenced objects. The *finalize()* method is run only once by the GC before it cleans up the object automatically even though there is no particular reason to clean up all your objects using this method.	→ It does necessary cleanup operations such as unsetting internal class objects, closing database connections or socket connections, etc. → The destructor is automatically called when an object should be destroyed. An object is ready for destroy when, object goes out of scope, object set to null, unsetting or the program execution is over. → The destructor will be called even after executing exit(). → In PHP, *__destruct* is used invoke the destructor.
Syntax of Destructor	`~NameOfClass(){  }`	Java is a garbage collected language, hence there is no explicit destructor is specified. Still if you need to perform some additional tasks w.r.t clean up the memory, then you can use the *finalize()* method.	`function __destruct(){}`

Example of Destructor			
| | ```
class Test {
public:
char* name;
Test(const char* n)
{
cout<<"In constructor
of Test"<<endl;
name= strcpy(new
char[strlen(n) + 1],
n);
}
~Test(){
cout<<"In destroying
of"<<name;
delete[] name;
}
};
int main(){
Test t("Test");
return 0;
}
``` | finalize() does not guarantee of execution because it depends on Garbage Collector(GC). In some cases, GC may never be invoked during the lifetime of the program. Example of finalize() method is given below,

```
class Test {
public static
int obj =0 ;
public String name;
public Test
(String name)
{
this.name = name;
obj++;
}
protected void
finalize()
{
obj--;
System.out.println
("finalizing...");
}
}
class Test1{
public static
void main
(String[] args)
{
Test obj = new
Test("Test");
}
}
``` | ```
<?php
class Test {
function __construct() {
print"Constructing Test"
."\n";
$this->name = "Test";
}
function __destruct() {
print "Destroying " .
$this->name ;
}
}
$obj = new Test();
?>
``` |

Chapter 12

Packages(Namespaces)

The term used for C++, PHP is *Namespaces* and for Java it is *Packages*, the main intention of using packages/namespace is to group related files/classes logically, to avoid name conflicts, etc.

12.1 PACKAGES

Features	C++	Java	PHP
What is Packages (Namespaces)?	Namespaces defines a context or scope or subscope for names. It basically allow to group entities like classes, objects and functions under a name. Hence namespace helps to overcome the difficulty of repetitive names or provides additional information to differentiate similar functions, classes, variables etc. with the same name available in different libraries.	A package in Java is a namespace that organizes a set of related classes, interfaces, enumerations and annotations. This will help to prevent naming conflicts, to control access, to make searching/locating and usage of related types. The Java platform provides an enormous class library (a set of packages like java.lang, java.io etc) suitable for any applications.	The logic of namespace is smiler to C++. Namespaces allow ambiguous related types with same name where group related types are classes, interfaces, functions and constants. Namespaces in PHP helps to solve name collisions between internal PHP classes/functions/constants and/or third-party classes/functions/constants, ability to alias (or shorten) *Extra_Long_Names* to improve readability of source code.

	The keyword *using* is used to specify a name from a namespace into the current declarative region, we normally use statement like *using namespace std;*, which means all the files in the C++ standard library declare all of its entities within the *std* namespace(iostream).	When a package name is not specified, a class will be placed into the default package (the current working directory) and the package itself is given no name. To create an object (usage of package) of a class belongs to a package, you have to use its fully qualified name in the import syntax import [package name with optional class name], e.g, import p1.p2.event.*; Java package declaration should be written before any other *import* statements. The name of the package becomes a part of the name of the class, the name of the package must match the directory structure where the corresponding bytecode resides. The advantages of Java packages includes flexibility compare to C++, classes can be easily determined and use related files, avoids name conflicts, it allows types within the package to have unrestricted access to one another yet still restrict access for types outside the package. In some cases, it is required to set your CLASSPATH so that the compiler and the JVM can find the .class files for your types.	Namespaces are declared using the *namespace* keyword. A file containing a *namespace* must declare the namespace at the top of the file before any other code except *declare* construct. Without assigning name to namespace is treated as *global namespace*.

Syntax	`namespace identifier`
	`{`
	`entities`
	`}`
		`package identifier;`
		`class{`
		`}`
			`<?php`
			`namespace {Optional`
			`NameOfNamespace} {`
			`//Global space if`
			`//no namespace.`
			`}`

Example	`namespace` `TestNameSpace` `{` `   int varX,varY;` `}` `The namespaces is` `useful in the case` `where a global` `object or function` `uses the same` `identifier as another` `one, causing` `redefinition errors.` `Example:` `#include <iostream>` `using namespace std;` `namespace Test1` `{` `int size = 101;` `int length = 11;` `}` `namespace Test2` `{` `long size = 1000001;` `long length = 11111;` `}` `int main () {` `using Test1::size;` `using Test2::length;` `cout << size<< endl;` `cout << length<< endl;` `cout<<Test1::length` `<<endl;` `cout<<Test2::` `size<<endl;` `return 0;` `}` `Output:` `101` `11111` `11` `1000001`	`file name: ABC.java` `package Test;` `class ABC{` `public void method(){` `System.out.` `println("Hi");` `}` `}` `file name: DEF.java` `package Test.Test1;` `class DEF{` `public void method(){` `System.out.println` `("Hello");` `}` `}` `file name: C.java` `import Test.*;` `class C{` `public static` `void main` `(String args[]){` `   Test.Test1 obj = new` `   Test.Test1.DEF();` `   obj.method();` `  }` `}` `Output:` `Hello`	`file1:` `<?php namespace test1;` `class ABC {` `static function method()` `{echo 'test1';}  } ?>` `file2:` `<?php namespace test2;` `class DEF {` `static function method()` `{echo 'test2';}  } ?>` `file3:` `<?php namespace test3;` `class GHI {` `static function method1()` `{echo 'test3';}  } ?>` `file4:` `<?php namespace test4;` `include 'file1.php';` `include 'file2.php';` `include 'file3.php';` `use test1 as temp1;` `use test2 as temp2;` `use test3;` `echo \temp1\ABC::` `method(), " \n";` `echo \temp2\DEF::` `method(), " \n";` `echo \test3\GHI::` `method1(), " \n";` `?>` `Output:` `test1` `test2` `test3`

Chapter 13

Exceptions

An exception is a problem or a bug that arises during the execution of a program and transfer control to another module or program. An exception can arise in many cases, like invalid data, resource not found, connection lost, memory issue, invalid business logic etc.

13.1 EXCEPTIONS

C++, Java and PHP languages use try, catch and throw keywords for exception handling, in addition to these, Java and PHP has *finally* block for cleanup process.

When an exception is thrown, code following the statement will not be executed, and interpretor will attempt to find the first matching *catch* block.

try: A try block holds business logic or a block of code for which particular exceptions will be evaluated followed by one or more catch blocks.

catch: If any exception arise in *try* block, then such exception needs to catch as an exception with an exception handler, you can use as many *catch* blocks as you need in the application.

throw: A throw statement or expression is used to throw exceptions to exception handlers.

finally: If try block is executed then finally block will automatically executes. If you write return as the last statement in the try block and no exception occurs, the finally block will still execute. After finally block execution only return statement executes.

Exceptions can be thrown (or re-thrown) within a catch block. You can create a custom exception handler.

Features	C++	Java	PHP

Syntax			
	``
try
{
    // business code
}catch(ExceptionName
 e1)
{
    throw expression;
}catch(ExceptionName
e2)
{
    // catch block
}catch(ExceptionName
eN)
{
    // catch block
}
``` There is a special catch called catch all that can catch all kind of exceptions.

Example:
```
catch (...) {
cerr << "Exception
thrown..."<< endl;
}
```

All exceptions are unchecked.
Resource Acquisition Is Initialization(RAII) is used in C++ similar to *finally*.
Example:

```
void abc()
{
std::unique_ptr<T>t
(new T)
try
  {
//code that uses t
}
catch (...)
{
}
}
```

Unhanded exceptions that is not caught by handlers will call *std::terminate* which will call abort with a signal *SIGABRT* and then entire program will be terminated. | ```
try
{
//business code
}catch(ExceptionType1
e1)
{
//Catch block
}catch(ExceptionType2
e2)
{
//Catch block
}catch(ExceptionType3
e3)
{
//Catch block
}finally
{
//The finally block
// always executes.
}
```

There are two types of exceptions i.e, checked and unchecked.
throws keyword is used to list exceptions that can be thrown by a method.
Catch All can be achieved using Base exception, e.g,
catch (Exception e)

Unhanded exceptions that is not caught by handlers will print a stack trace and terminate the thread. Java programmer may provide an *UncaughtException* handler.
Exceptions can be thrown (or re-thrown) in a catch block within a *try* block.
JVM Exceptions/errors are exclusively or logically thrown by the JVM, e.g, NullPointerException, ArrayIndexOutOf-BoundsException, ClassCastException. | ```
try
{
//business code
}catch(ExceptionType1
$e1)
{
//Catch block
}catch(ExceptionType2
$e2)
{
//Catch block
}catch(ExceptionType3
$e3)
{
//Catch block
}finally
{
//The finally block
// always executes.
}
```

Exceptions can be thrown (or re-thrown) in a catch block within a *try* block.
*finally* is similar to Java's *finally* block.
*Exception* is the base class for all Exceptions. |
```

		Programmatic exceptions are thrown explicitly by the application or the API programmers, e.g., IllegalArgumentException, IllegalStateException. *Checked exceptions* is typically a user error or a problem that cannot be foreseen by the programmer. *Runtime exceptions* occurs while running your program/application. As opposed to checked exceptions, runtime exceptions are ignored at the time of compilation. *Errors* are also unchecked exception and the programmer is not required to do anything with these issues e.g, OutOfMemoryError, StackOverflowError, etc. *finally* block is used to close files, recover resources, and otherwise clean up after the code enclosed in the try block. The try statement should contain at least one catch block or a finally block and may have multiple catch blocks. *Throwable* is the base class for all Exceptions.	

Example			
| | ```cpp
#include <iostream>
class Test{
public:
double div(int v1,
int v2)
{
if( v2== 0 ){
throw "div by zero!";
}
return (v1/v2);
}
};
int main ()
{
int a= 10;
int b= 0;
double c= 0;
Test t;
try {
c= t.div(a, b);
cout << c << endl;
}catch (const char*
str)
{
cerr << str<< endl;
}
catch (...) {
cerr << "Exception
thrown..."<< endl;
    }
return 0;
}
Output:
div by zero!
``` | ```java
class Test{
double div(int a,
int b)
 throws Exception
{
if( b == 0 )
{
throw new Exception
("div by zero!");
}
return (a/b);
}
public static void
main (String str[])
{
int x = 10;
int y = 0;
double z = 0;
Test t = new Test();
try {
z = t.div(x, y);
System.out.println(z);
}catch (Exception
str1){
System.out.println
(str1);
}
}
}
Output:
ArithmeticException
div by zero!
``` | ```php
<?php
class Test{
function div1( $a,   $b)
{
if( $b == 0 )
{
throw new Exception
 "div by zero!";
}
return ($a/$b);
}
}
$x = 10;
$y = 0;
$z = 0;
$t = new Test();
try {
$z = $t->div1($x, $y);
System.out.println($z);
}catch (Exception $e) {
echo $e->getMessage();
}
?>
Output: PHP Parse error:
syntax error, unexpected
'"div by zero!"'
``` |
```

Chapter 14

Files

File is a data file which can be opened and closed for reading and/or writing operations.

14.1 FILES

A file must be opened before you can read from it or write to it, but before that, it should be created. When application terminated or after end of execution, then program automatically flushes all the streams, release all the allocated memory and close all the opened files. However it is always a good practice to release all the connections before program termination.

A *stream* can be defined as a sequence of data.

Features	C++	Java	PHP
Description	Header files *iostream* and *fstream* is required for file processing. *ofstream or fstream* object may be used to open a file for writing purpose and *ifstream* object is used to open a file for reading purpose only. File position pointers, *seekg("seek get")* for *istream* and *seekp("seek put")* for *ostream* provide member functions for repositioning the file position pointer which is an integer value that specifies the location in the file as a number of bytes from the file's starting location. Example(setting ios::beg): fileObject.seekg (startingPos); fileObject.seekg (startingPos, ios::cur); fileObject.seekg (startingPos, ios::end); fileObject.seekg (0, ios::end);	The *InputStream* is used to read data from a source and the *OutputStream* is used for writing data to a target. Statement used for storing character based stream in BufferReader from console input is, *BufferedReader buff = new BufferedReader(new InputStream-Reader(System.in));*. Now we can use a method called *read()* to get a character or *readLine()* method to read a string from the console. *FileInputStream*(used for reading data from the files) and *FileOutputStream*(used to create a file and write data into it) are used for file operations.	The fopen() function opens a file or URL. If fopen() gets any exception, it returns FALSE and an error on failure, errors can be hidden by adding an '' in front of the function name.

Syntax	Opening a File:
	`void open(const char *filename, ios::openmode mode | ios::openmode mode ...);`
	openmode can be, ios::app(append mode), ios::ate(move the read/write control to the EOF), ios::in(read), ios::out(write), ios::trunc(truncate content).
	
	Closing a File:
	`void close();`
		Reading data from file:
		`InputStream fl=new FileInputStream (fileNameWithPath);`
		or
		`File fl = new File (fileNameWithPath); InputStream fstream = new FileInputStream (fl);`
		
		Operations on the input stream:read(int r), read(byte[] r), available(), finalize(), close(). Other input streams are supported in Java are *ByteArrayInputStream* and *DataInputStream*.
		
		Create a file and/or write data into it:
		`OutputStream fl = new FileOutputStream (fileNameWithPath) ;`
		or
		`File fl = new File (fileNameWithPath); OutputStream fstream = new FileOutputStream (fl);`
		
		Operations on the output stream:write(int w), write(byte[] w), finalize(), close(). Other output streams are supported in Java are *ByteArrayOutputStream* and *DataOutputStream*.
			`resource = fopen( filename,mode, include_path,context);`
			
			filename: File or URL to open and it is mandatory.
			mode: Type of access on file/stream and it is mandatory. Possible values of mode are,
			"r" (Read only): Starts at the beginning of the file.
			"r+" (Read/Write): Starts at the beginning of the file.
			"w" (Write only): Opens and clears the contents of file; or creates a new file if it doesn't exist.
			"w+" (Read/Write): Opens and clears the contents of file; or creates a new file if it doesn't exist.
			"a" (Write only): Opens and writes to the end of the file or creates a new file if it doesn't exist.
			"a+" (Read/Write): Preserves file content by writing to the end of the file.
			"x" (Write only): Creates a new file. Returns FALSE and an error if file already exists.
			"x+" (Read/Write): Creates a new file. Returns FALSE and an error if file already exists.
			
			include_path: It is optional value.Value '1' indicates to search for the file in the include_path.
			context: It is Optional and specifies the context of the file handle which helps to modify the behaviour of a stream.
			resource: Returns a file pointer resource on success, or FALSE on error.
			It is important to note that while writing to a text file, be sure to use the correct line-ending character!

Example			

	Opening a File:
	fileStream.open(
	"file.dat",
	ios::out | ios::in);
	Closing a File:
	fileStream.close();
	
	Program Example:
	
	#include <fstream>
	#include <iostream>
	int main ()
	{
	char arr[100];
	ofstream fileOut;
	fileOut.open(
	"Test.dat");
	cin.getline(arr,100);
	fileOut << arr
	<< endl;
	cout
	<< "Enter a Number";
	cin >> arr;
	cin.ignore();
	fileOut <<arr<<endl;
	fileOut.close();
	ifstream fileIn;
	fileIn.open
	("Test.dat");
	fileIn >> arr;
	cout << arr << endl;
	fileIn >> arr;
	cout << arr << endl;
	fileIn.close();
	return 0;
	}
		import java.io.*;
		class Test{
		public static void
		main(String args[]){
		try{
		byte wdata [] =
		{1,2,3};
		OutputStream fos = new
		FileOutputStream(
		"C:/file1.txt");
		for(int i=0; i <
		wdata.length ; i++){
		fos.write(wdata[i]);
		}
		fos.close();
		InputStream fis =
		new FileInputStream
		("C:/file1.txt");
		int size =
		fis.available();
		for(int i=0; i<
		size; i++){
		System.out.print(
		(char)fis.read()
		+ " ");
		}
		fis.close();
		}catch(IOException
		e){
		}
		}
		}
			<?php
			$fs = fopen("test.txt",
			"r");
			$fs = fopen("/home/fs/
			test.txt","r");
			$fs = fopen("/home/fs/
			test.gif","wb");
			$fs = fopen("http://
			www.google.com/","r");
			$fs = fopen("/home/fs/
			test1.txt","w");
			$fs = fopen("c:\\fs\\
			res.txt", "r");
			?>

Chapter 15

Data Base Connection

In some instances where we need to access different Data Bases from different vendors like Oracle, MYSQL, DB2 etc.

15.1   DATA BASE CONNECTION

Features	C++	Java	PHP
Description	There are many third parties has implemented the wrapper classes over Database and C++ integration.	The JDBC is a Java API defines interfaces and classes for reading/writing database applications in Java by making database connections.	Here we are taking MySQL as Database for connection. The function used to connect the database is called *mysql_connect()*. This function returns a resource or handle which is a pointer to the database connection. *mysql_select_db()* is used to connect a DataBase. *mysql_query()* is used to get the records through query. *mysql_close* is used to close the database connection.

Example: SOCI, MFC Database classes, ATL Database classes, MSDN DAP, ORCACLE's OCCI etc. You can refer there APIs documentation to access DB resources.	Steps to get connected DB, a) Register the database driver: *Class.forName(specific DB driver classs);* b) Create a database connection: *Connection conn = DriverManager.getConnection(url, username, password);* c) Create a query: *PreparedStatement stm= Conn.prepareStatement(SQL query);* d) Exceute the query : *stm.exceuteUpdate();*	Example: ```<?php $username = "oralce1"; $password = "oracle123"; $hostname = "localhost"; $handle =mysql_connect ($hostname, $username, $password) or die("Unable to connect to MySQL"); echo "Connected..."; $selected=mysql_select_db ("DB1",$handle) or die("Could not select DB1"); $result = mysql_query("SELECT id, name, date FROM table1"); mysql_close($handle); ?>```

Chapter 16

Memory Management

Memory management is very important feature of every programming language, this can be done manually or automatically.

16.1 MEMORY MANAGEMENT

In manual memory management, memory is controlled by the developer e.g., C++. In automatic memory management, Garbage Collection is used to deallocate memory automatically when control flow goes to out of scope, e.g., Java.

C++	Java	PHP
Dynamic memory can be allocated and deallocated by using *new, new[]* and *delete, delete[]* operator respectively. After allocation, *new* returns a pointer to the beginning of the new block of memory allocated. Syntax: Allocate memory to contain one single element of type *type*. `pointer = new type;` `delete pointer;`	Memory is allocated for local variable while method invocation time and deallocated when method returns. When we use *new* operator for memory allocation, then it takes from heap memory and deallocation will be done automatically. New objects created in heap irrespective of there scope e.g. local or member variable are released when it will become out of scope.	Memory is automatically allocated to a object when you instantiate it and it frees the memory when object destroyed/deleted. The process of cleaning up unreferenced objects is known as GC(Garbage Collection). The type of garbage collection used by PHP is called *Reference Counting(RC)*.

Allocate memory to assign a block (an array) of elements of type *type*, where numOfElements is an integer value representing the amount of memory.
 	
```\npointer = new type\n[numOfElements];\ndelete [] pointer;\n```
 	
Example:
 	
```\nMemory for Variable:\nInt *var= new int[10];\ndelete [] var;\n```
 	
```\nMemory for Object:\nTestClass *obj =\nnew TestClass();\ndelete obj;\n```
 	
nothrow is used to hide the exception related to memory allocation.
Example:
int * p;
p= new (nothrow) int[100];
	GC will reclaim the heap space from objects which are eligible for Garbage collection via running a daemon thread called Garbage Collector.
	Example:List arr = new ArrayList();
	Garbage collector will clear the memory when object in not referenced. Before removing an object from memory Garbage collection thread invokes finalize () method. *System.gc () and Runtime.gc ()* is used to send request of Garbage collection to JVM but its not guaranteed that garbage collection will happen and also it is not good practice to use it.
	If sufficient memory is not available for creating new object in Heap, JVM throws OutOfMemoryError or java.lang.OutOfMemoryError
		RC records existence of string, number, object etc and sets a counter to one for each, indicating that there's one copy of the value to track it and also it increments and decrements its counter accordingly whenever reference it and *unset* it respectively.
		RC increment by one when you create a reference to the value, either by passing it into a function by reference or by assigning it by reference to another variable. Similarly Reference Counting decrement by one when you remove a reference to a value, which happens when you exit a function or delete the variable.
		Example:
		
		```\n$animal = new Cat();\n// New object:RC = 1\nanimal1 = $animal;\n// Copy-by-reference:RC= 2\nunset($animal);\n// Delete a reference:RC = 1\nunset(animal1);\n// Delete a reference:RC = 0\n```
		
		When RC reaches zero, PHP knows the object is no longer used anywhere in the program, now object's destructor will be called to clean up any higher-level resources you have opened for the object, then deletes the object and releases its memory, finally PHP cleans up all the remaining values that still have a nonzero reference count at the end of execution.

Chapter 17

FAQs

In this section, Frequently Asked Questions(FAQ) are described for C++, Java and PHP.

17.1   C++ FAQS

What is C++?
C++ is a Object Oriented Language comprises both high-level and low-level language features which is developed by Bjarne Stroustrup starting in 1979 at Bell Labs.

What is Object Oriented Programming?
It is a programming model where program uses object to access fields and methods.

What is the difference between procedural(POP) and object-oriented programs(OOP)?
Procedural programming is a top down approach and object oriented programs is a bottom up approach. Logic of procedural programming follows certain procedures and the instructions are executed one after another where as in OOP program, unit of program is a object which is a combination of fields and methods. In POP, data is exposed to the whole program whereas in OOP, it is accessible within the object and assures the security of the code.

What is a main() method in C++?
main() is a starting point of program execution. This function implicitly returns 0 to compiler while completing the program execution.

What is default parameter?

This is used when a parameter should have a specified value and the caller does not supply a value that parameter. Example:

```
void method(int x=15){
//code
}
main()
{
method(10); // Passes 10 to method()
method(); // Passes 15 to method()
}
```

What is virtual members?

Virtual members A member of a class that can be redefined in its subclass/derived classes is known as a virtual member, to make virtual member, precede its declaration with the keyword *virtual*.

Example:

```
#include <iostream>
class Test {
  protected:
    int x, y;
  public:
    void setMethod (int c, int d)
      { x=c; y=d; }
    virtual int method () //virtual method
      { return (0); }
};

class Test1: public Test {
  public:
    int method ()
      { return (x * y*10); }
};

class Test2: public Test {
  public:
    int method ()
      { return (x * y / 10); }
};

int main () {
//method calling
}
```

What is pure virtual function?

This is used to not to specify any implementation for the function. All classes that contain at least one pure virtual function are abstract base classes.

Example: virtual int method () =0;

What is difference between abstract base class and a regular polymorphic class?
The main difference between an abstract base class and a regular polymorphic class is that because in abstract base classes at least one of its members does not have implementation so cannot create a instances (objects) of it.

What is difference between stack memory and heap memory?
Stack memory(temporary region of memory)is used for local variable for temporaries, stack pointer pushed on function entry and popped on function exit.   Heap memory(dynamically allocated memory) is distinct region of memory for persistent objects, this memory is usually allocate when we use *new* keyword. This memory can be released by the programmer(*delete* operator).

Why virtual constructor doesn't exist in C++?
Constructor is used for creating an instance of a class and it cant be delegated to any other object by using *virtual* keyword.

Is virtual destructor used in C++?
We can use a virtual destructor at runtime depending on the type of object pointer is pointing to.

What is deference between *realloc* and *free*?
The *free* function is used to release the memory block allocated by malloc or calloc or realloc. The *realloc* function is used change the size of memory block, this function not only increase the size but data is remain unchanged.

Why array always starts from index 0 in C++?
Array name in C++ is a constant pointer pointing to the base address of the memory allocated. Example:Say array declaration *arr[i]*, then compiler manipulates it as *(arr + i)*. The value of *i* must be 0 for accessing it since *arr* is the address of the first element.

What is difference between Array and Vector?
The size of an Array is fixed in declaration whereas Vector is also an Array but the size of a Vector can change dynamically.

Can you allocate the memory using *malloc()*(C Language)and deallocate the same memory using *delete*(C++ Language)?
You can delete memory created by *malloc()* by using *free()* without any problem and similarly new/delete combination too. However memory created using *malloc()* cant be deleted using *delete* and similarly for new/free() combination too.

What scope resolution operator?
This is used to resolve the name conflicts of local and global scope. For example if an identifier in the global scope that has been hidden by another identifier with the same name in the local scope.

What is difference between this and friend operator?
this pointer points to the current object of the class. A *friend* function is used to access the private members of the class by using *friend* keyword preceding to it while declaring and not while defining. Friend function can be declared as either as private or as public inside the class.

What is function overloading and operator overloading?
Function overloading is nothing but using same name for several functions with similar task comprising of different type of parameters, the C++ compiler selects the proper function by examining the number of parameters, types and order of the arguments in the call. In Operator overloading, operators to be redefined so that they work on objects of user-defined classes.

What is the difference between a copy constructor and an overloaded assignment operator?

A copy constructor used to form a new object by using the content of the argument object where as overloaded assignment operator assigns the contents of an existing object to another object of the same class.

What is the difference between declaration and definition?

The declaration informs to the compiler about a method with optional parameters saying that at some later point of time we plan to implement the definition of this declaration.
```
Example: void method () //function declaration
```

```
The definition gives the actual implementation.
```

```
Example: void method () // function declaration
{
//body of the function
}
```

What is Dangling Pointer?

It is a pointer which is pointing to an object which no longer exists.
```
Example:
Test* t(new Test);
Test* r = t;
delete t;
t->method(); // p is now dangling!
t = NULL; // p is no longer dangling
```

What are the advantages of inheritance?

It gives re-usability of code and it saves time in the program development. It gives functional hierarchy.

What is difference between NULL and 0?

In C++, NULL is 0, so there is only an aesthetic difference. NULL is usually used for object and 0 is used as numeric value.

What do you mean by inline function?

This function is used to insert the code of a called function at the point where the function is called to improve the application's performance in exchange for increased compile time and possibly an increase in the size of the generated binary executables.

Which is faster ++i(Pre-increment) or i++(Post-increment)?
i++ is slower than ++i, please see below justification. In ++i, first the variable is incremented and new value is returned, hence it requires one instruction to increment the variable. In i++, the old value has to be returned or used in the expression and then the variable is incremented after the expression is evaluated. Since you need one instruction to save the old value to be used in the expression and other instruction to increment the variable.

What is memory leak?
Memory which has objects with no reference pointing to it and there is no way to delete or reuse this memory(object) hence it causes memory leak.

What is the difference between an Array and a List?
Array is collection of homogeneous elements. where as list is collection of heterogeneous elements. Memory allocated for array is static and continuous where as for list, it is dynamic and Random. In array, user need not have to track next memory allocation, where as in list, user has to keep track of next location where memory is allocated. Array uses direct access of stored members, where as list uses sequential access for members.

What is a template?

Templates used to create generic functions that admit any data type as parameters and return value without having to overload the function with all the possible data types.
Syntax:
 	
`template <class indetifier> function_declaration;`
`template <typename indetifier> function_declaration;`

What is encapsulation?
It is OOP feature to wrapping up of data and functions into a single unit (called class).

What are memory management operations?

The *new* and *delete* are preprocessors while *malloc()* and *free()* are functions.

In *new* operation, no need of allocating the size of memory and initialize new memory to 0 where as in case of *malloc()*, we have to use *sizeof()* and also it assigns random values(to avoid this, use *calloc*) for allocated memory.

The *new* allocates continuous space for the object instance, where as *malloc()* allocates distributed space.

The *new* cannot cast because it allocates memory for this specific type, where as *malloc()*, *calloc()* allocate space for void * that is casted to the specific class type pointer.

The *calloc* reserves storage space and initialize memory to 0.

The *free( )* is used to release the memory which is allocated by *malloc()* or *calloc()*. *delete/delete[ ]* is used to release the memory which is allocated by *new/new[ ]*. *free( )* is used in C, where *delete/delete[ ]* is used in C++.

Don't use *malloc( )*, or *calloc( )* with *delete/delete[]*, and don't use *new/new[]* with *free()*.

What is the use of enumerated data type?

It is a another user defined type which provides a way for attaching names to numbers thereby increasing comprehensibility of the code. The *enum* keyword automatically enumerates a list of words by assigning them values 0,1,2,3 and so on.

What is the difference between class and structure?

The *structure* is used to bundle different type of data types and functions(default:public) together to perform a particular functionality.

The class is a enhancement or successor of *structure*. By default all the members inside the class are private.

What is abstraction?

It is a process of hiding unwanted details from the user.

What is the difference between Object and Instance?

Both words are used interchangeably for representing the class object. An object is an instance of a class, instance of a user defined type is called an object.

What is the difference between an external iterator(EI) and an internal iterator(II)?

An II is developed with member functions of the class that has items to step through. An EI is developed as a separate class that can be tied to the object that has items to step through, many different iterators can be actived simultaneously on the same object.

What is the difference between macro and iniine?

Macros does not follows strict parameter type checking and always expanded by preprocessor but inline is strictly type based and compiler may or may not replace the inline definitions.

---

what is reference variable?

It provides an alias to a previously defined variable.
Example:
```
DataType & reference-name = variable-name;
```

What is *extern* keyword?

To use function outside the file in which it is defined, *extern* is used. Variable or function may be defined in another file, declaration is used to describe the variable/function that is externally defined.

What is implicit conversion?

If you have mixed data types in an expression then c++ performs the conversion automatically.
Example : In the expression of integer and float, then integer is converted into float type. Smaller type is converted to wider type.

What is the difference between char c[] = "abc"; and char *s = "abc";?

In *c[]*, 3 bytes are allocated to the variable *c* which is fixed, where as in *s*, if it is assigned to some other value, then allocated memory can change.

What are virtual functions?
The virtual functions should be members of some class and it cannot be static member. These functions are accessed by using object pointers and it can be a friend of another class.

What are storage qualifiers in C++ ?
const: Once memory is initialized, should not be altered by a program. *volatile*: The value in the memory location can be altered even though nothing in the program. *mutable*: Particular member of a structure or class can be altered even if a particular structure variable, class, or class member function is constant.

When template is a better solution than a base class?
While designing a generic class to contain or otherwise manage objects of other types, when the format and behaviour of those other types are unimportant to their containment or management, and particularly when those other types are unknown to the designer of the container or manager class.

What is dynamic/late binding(run time)?
The code associated with a given procedure call is not known until the time of the call at run time due to object association with polymorphism and inheritance.

What do you mean by early binding?
This refers to the events that occur at compile time, it occurs when all information needed to call a function is known at the compile time. For examples, normal function calls, overloaded function calls, and overloaded operators. Early binding is having more efficiency than late binding.

What is *explicit* constructor?

It is a conversion constructor declared with the *explicit* keyword to be ignored by compiler as its purpose is reserved explicitly for construction.

What is dynamic constructor?

Dynamic constructor used to allocate memory while creating objects using *new* keyword, allocation of memory to objects at the time of their construction is known as dynamic construction of objects.

What is the use of "using" declaration?

Used to get a name from a namespace.

What is an accessor?

It is a class operation that does not modify the state of an object, this need to be declared as *const* operations.

What is a container class? What are the types of container classes?

A container class is a generic holder class that is used to hold objects in memory or external storage. It has a predefined behaviour and a well known interface. A container class is a helping class whose purpose is to hide the topology used for maintaining the list of objects in memory. When a container class contains a group of mixed objects, the container is called as a *heterogeneous* container; when the container is holding a group of objects that are all the same, the container is called a *homogeneous* container.

What is incomplete type?

It is refers to pointers in which there is non availability of the implementation of the referenced location or it points to some location whose value is not available for modification.
Example:
int *j=0x1000 // j points to address 1000
*j=0; //set the value of memory location pointed by j.
Incomplete types are otherwise called uninitialized pointers.

Differentiate between the message and method.
A message is between Objects for communication purpose and it is sent to invoke a method. A method is basically a implementation of an operation which provides a response to a message

What is an Adaptor class or Wrapper class?
A class that has no functionality of its own and its member functions hide the use of a third party software component or an object with the non-compatible interface or a non-object-oriented implementation.

What is problem with Runtime type identification?
It is performance penalty.

What is a Null object?
It indicate that a real object of the class does not exist or failed to get instance of the class.

What is the use of storage class specifiers?
It is used to refine the declaration of a variable, a function and parameters. The storage class specifiers are, auto, register, static and extern.

What is class invariant?
It is a logical condition that defines all valid states for an object. This will hold the details about when an object is created, and they must be preserved under all operations of the class. All class invariants are both preconditions and post-conditions for all operations or member functions of the class.

What are proxy objects/surrogates?
Objects that stand for other objects are called proxy objects.

What is stack unwinding?
It is a process during exception handling when the destructor is called for all local objects between the place where the exception was thrown and where it is caught.

What is a modifier/mutators?
It is a member function that changes the value of at least one data member or it modifies the state of an object.

What is STL(Standard Template Library)? and what are the components of STL?
A collection of generic classes and functions is called as Standard Template Library (STL) and its components are containers, algorithm and iterators.

How can we access protected and private members of a class?
The protected and private members cannot be accessed from outside the same class at which they are declared. But this can be achieved with the use of the *friend* keyword in a class, so we can allow an external function to gain access to the protected and private members of a class.

17.2 JAVA FAQS

What is JAVA?
In 1995, Sun Microsystems (ORACLE acquired) has released a programming language called JAVA.JAVA is computing platform used to write utilities like, games, and business applications etc.

Why JAVA?
Java is platform independent, fast, secure, reliable and runs over the WWW.

What is a classpath?
It is a path where Java looks for loading class at run time and compile time.

What is a path?
It is a location where the OS will look for finding out the executable files and commands.

What are the advantages (features) of JAVA?
1. Platform independent (Multi-platform supporting language). 2. Object oriented language 3. It is an open source. 4. Supports garbage collection, hence memory management is automatic. 5. Used for dynamic web applications. 6. Used to create modular programs and reusable codes. 7. Robust and Secure. 8. Multithreaded.

When you will get java.lang.NullPointerException ?

1) Accessing Object is NULL or you haven't initialized Object.
2) Accessing an array beyond the Size of array.
Example:
`String str=null;`
`if (str.equals(abc))`
`    method();`

Why garbage collection is required?
This is used to identify the unused objects or a program no longer needs that so that their resources can be reclaimed and reused. If Object becomes unreachable to the program then that object is eligible for garbage collection. Garbage collection will reduce the burden of freeing allocated memory for programmers. Example: System.gc();

What is a Class?

A Java class is a group of Java methods and variables, it act as a blueprint or prototype or template from which objects are created. A class defines the state and behavior of a real-world object. A class can extend only one another class but it can implement one or more interfaces.

1. A class can have modifiers such as public and private.

2. A class should have name of class.

3. The class body, surrounded by braces, .

4. The name of baseclass, if any, proceeded by the keyword extends. A class can only extend (subclass) one parent.

5. A comma-separated list of interfaces implemented by the class, if any, preceded by the keyword implements. A class can implement more than one interface.

Example:

```
public class Area {//class
//Members like methods, constructors and variables
}
```

What is an Object?

Software objects are similar to real-world objects. Software objects are often used to model the real-world objects that you find in everyday life with state and behaviour.

Example:

```
public class Area {
  private int sqarea(int side){
    int area = side * side;
    return(area);
  }
  public static void main(String[] args){
Area a=new Area ();//Object creation
System.out.println(a.sqarea(100));
  }
}
Output:
10000
```

What is an Interface?

An interface is a named collection of method definitions but without implementations (abstract methods). An interface can also include constant declarations. Interface methods are always instance methods. If you want to use them, there must be some associated object that implements the interface. You cant instantiate an interface directly, but you can instantiate a class that implements an interface. References to an Object can by via the class name, via one of its superclass names, or one of its interface names.
Interface rules,
1. An interface can extend one of more interfaces but cannot extend class and cannot implement any interface.
2. You can declare static constant (final) variables in interfaces.
3. All its methods in the interface are abstract methods implicitly, no static methods are allowed.
4. No static initialiser blocks allowed inside of interface.
5. The throws clauses about Exceptions in the interfaces methods must exactly match the throws clauses of the implementing methods in the classes.
Example:
```
interface Inter1{
public void method1();
}
interface Inter2 extends Inter1{
public void method2();
public  static final int val=100;
}
public class Test implements Inter2{

public void method1(){
System.out.println("Hello method1 !");
}
public void method2(){
System.out.println("Hello method2 !");
}

public static void main(String args[]){
Test test = new Test();
test.method1();
test.method2();
System.out.println("val= "+Inter2.val);
}
}
Output:
Hello method1 !
Hello method2 !
val= 100
```

What is synchronization?

Synchronization will come into picture when multithreading is used; synchronization is the capability to control the access of multiple threads to shared resources. If multiple threads are accessing same variable, then they have access it one by one.
Example:
```
public synchronized void method()
{
// Body of method
}
```

What are different ways of using threads?

A thread can be implemented by using runnable interface or by inheriting from the Thread class.
Example:

```
1) import java.lang.*;
public class ABCThread extends Thread
{
        public void run()
        {
        ....
        }
}


2)import java.lang.*;
public class ABCThread implements Runnable
{
        Thread T;
        public void run()
        {
        ....
        }
}
```

What is a Thread?

Thread is a program's execution path.

What is Process?

It is an instance of a program running in a system.

Is JAVA Pass by reference OR Pass by value?

Java supports Pass by value and not Pass by reference. In Pass by value ,a copy of the value to be passed, where as Pass by reference means , passing the address itself. In Java, arguments are always passed by value hence Java only supports pass by value. In Java, the object reference itself is passed by value and so both the original reference and parameter copy both will refer to the same object. Java primitives are also passed by value.

Example:

```java
public class test {
private String str="";
test(String st){
str=st;
}
public String getstr() {
    return str;
}
public void foo(test d) {
    d = new test("XYZ");
    System.out.println("foo:"+ d.getstr());
}
public static void main(String str[]){
test ABC = new test("TEST");
System.out.println("Before foo-ABC :"+ ABC .getstr());
ABC .foo(ABC);
System.out.println("After foo -ABC :"+ ABC .getstr());
}
}
OUTPUT:
Before foo-ABC :TEST
foo:XYZ
After foo -ABC :TEST
```

What is Map in JAVA?

Map is an interface, which is used to map keys to values. A map cannot contain duplicate keys, each key should map to at most one value. Map interface is part of java.util package. Map permits *null* value.

Example:

```java
import  java.util.Map;
import  java.util.Set;
import  java.util.HashMap;
import  java.util.Iterator;
public class MapTest{
    public static void main(String[] args) {
        Map<Object,String> intMap=new HashMap<Object, String>();
        // adding :Key->Value
        intMap.put(new Integer(108), "A");
        intMap.put(new Integer(78), "B");
        intMap.put(new Integer(98), "C");

        Set st=intMap.entrySet();
        Iterator valIt=st.iterator();

        while(valIt.hasNext())
        {
            Map.Entry mp =(Map.Entry)valIt.next();
            int ky=(Integer)mp.getKey();
            String val=(String)mp.getValue();
            System.out.println("Key :"+ky+"  Value :"+val);
        }
    }
}

OUTPUT:
Key :78    Value :B
Key :108   Value :A
Key :98    Value :C
```

What is HashMap?
Hashmap is a class that implements Map .

What is Iterators?

java.util.Iterator is an Interface which allows you to walk through a collection of objects, operating on each object in turn. During using of Iterators that they contain a snapshot of the collection at the time the Iterator was obtained; it is not advisable to modify the collection itself while traversing an Iterator.
Highlights,
The Iterator interface is used to walk through the elements of a Collection.
Iterators let you process each element of a Collection.
Iterators are a generic way to go through all the elements of a Collection no matter how it is organized.
Example:

```
ArrayList<String> ABCList = new ArrayList<String>();
// Add Strings to ABCList
for (Iterator<String> it = ABCList.iterator(); it.hasNext(); ) {
    String str = it.next();
    System.out.println(str);
}
```

What is abstract class?
It is a class that is declared abstract; it may or may not include abstract methods. Abstract classes cannot be instantiated, but they can be subclassed. Abstract method is declared without an implementation. Example: abstract void add(double a, double b);

What is static method?

a)When a method is declared as static, it can be acccessed without creationg an object of the class and without referring to the object.
b)A static method belons to a class as a whole and not to any one instance/object of that class.All Static methods are implicitly final, because overriding is done based on the type of the object, and static methods are attached to a class, not an object.
c)A static method in a baseclass can be shadowed by another static method in a subclass, as long as the original method was not declared final. However, you can't override a static method with a nonstatic method.
d)A static method can only call other static methods.
e)A static method must only access static data.
f)A static method cannot reference to the current object using keywords super or this.
Example:
<code>public class MapTest{
  public static void staticCall(){
   System.out.println("This is static method ");
  }
 	
  public static void main(String[] args) {
   staticCall();
  }
}</code>

What is Final method?

A final keywork can be applied to methods, classes, data members, local variables and parameters depending on the context. A final class implicitly has all the methods as final, but not necessarily the data members. A final class may not be extended, neither may a final method be overridden.
Example:
```
public class ABC {
  public static final void foo() {
    System.out.println("foo()");
  }
}
```

What are Checked and UnChecked Exception?

Checked exceptions will force you to catch the exception and to do something about it based business need. These exceptions are meaningful and business might require it. Checked exceptions extend from Exception, methods should declare each checked exception it throws, caller to a method, which throws a checked exception, must either catch the exception or rethrow the exception itself.
Example:
```
    public class checkException extends Exception{
    }

    public class ABC {
    static {
    try {
    method();
    } catch (InterruptedException e) {
    throw new checkException();
    }
    }
    protected static void method() throws InterruptedException {
//method code
    }
    }
```
Unchecked exceptions are RuntimeException, which extend from either java.lang.RuntimeException or java.lang.Error.These exceptions could be unexpected.
Example:
```
public class runException extends RuntimeException {
    }

    public class ABC {
    static {
    try {
    method();
    } catch (InterruptedException e) {
    throw new runException();
    }
    }

    protected static void method() throws InterruptedException {
//method code
    }
    }
```

What is Overriding?

Overriding is used in modifying the methods of the super class or subclass method overriding a super class method. A subclass method will have same name, return type, and arguments as a method in its superclass.When the method is invoked for an object of the class, it is the new definition of the method that is called, and not the method definition from baseclass.
Rules to override the methods,
a)The return type should be the same.
b)Constructors cannot be overridden.
c)The argument list should be exactly the same as that of the overridden method.
d)Final method cannot be overridden.
e)static method cannot be overridden but can be re-declared.
f)Methods can be overridden only if they are inherited by the subclass.
g)The visibility cannot be more restrictive than the overridden method's access level.
h)Basically, if a method cannot be inherited then it cannot be overridden.
i)Constructors can be overloaded like regular methods.
Example:

```
class A{
    public void method(){
        System.out.println("A.method()");
    }
}
class B extends A{
    public void method(){
        super.method();
        System.out.println("B.method()");
    }
}
public class ABC{
    public static void main(String args[]){
        A b = new B();
        b.method();
    }
}
Output:
A.method()
B.method()
```

What is the default value of object declared as an instance variable?

null (if we dont define it explicitly)

What is serialization?

Serialization is a mechanism or process of converting a set of object instances that contain references to each other into a linear stream of bytes, which can then be transferred through a socket, stored to a file, or simply manipulated as a stream of data. This mechanism is used by RMI to pass objects between JVMs, either as arguments in a method invocation from a client to a server or as return values from a method invocation. If instances are to be serialized,then implement an interface Serializable, you pass the instance to the ObjectOutputStream which is connected to a fileoutputstream. It will save the object to a file. When you serialize an instance of a class, only non-static and non-transient instance data is saved, however Class definitions are not saved. It will be available when you try to deserialize an object.
Example:

```
class ABC implements Serializable {
 //members
}
```

What is Externalizable?

Externalizable is an Interface that extends Serializable Interface. It sends data into Streams in Compressed Format. Externalizable contains two methods readExternal() and writeExternal(). These methods will give you a control over the serialization mechanism and custom-written mechanisms to perform the marshalling and unmarshalling fuctions Thus if your class implements this interface, you can customize the serialization process by implementing these methods.
Example:

```
class ABC extends XYZ implements Externalizable {
    public void writeExternal( ObjectOutput out ) throws IOException {
//Method code
    }
    public void readExternal( ObjectInput in )
    throws IOException, ClassNotFoundException {
//Method code
    }
}
```

What is overloading in java?

Overloading is having more than one method with same name but different type of argument or differnt number of arguments available in same class or its subclass is called overloading. Return type and access specifier of method does not matter in method overloading.
Example:

```
class ABC{
    void add(int a,int b){    }
    void add (double a,double b){   }
    void add (float a, int b){ }
}
```

What is a transient variable?

The state of the variable will be always defaulted after the deserialisation,hence transient instance fields are neither saved nor restored by the standard serialization mechanism. Example:
Let variable ABCs value is set to 9999 , it's default value is '1' say, when the object has been serialized having ABCs value 9999, after deserialisation will be defaulted to '1'.

Where serialization is not applicable?

a) Transient Variables state will be always defaulted. b) Static Variables are not part of any particular state. c) Super class fields are only handled if the Super class itself is serializable.

What are wrapper classes?

Java wrappers are classes that wrap up primitive values in classes or converts into object, this is required in most of the collection classes. Java provides specialized classes corresponding to each of the primitive data types , eg., Integer, Character, Double etc. The wrapper classes also offer utility methods for converting to and from the int/float/double/char values they represent. All wrapper classes are all static so you can use them without creating an instance of the matching wrapper class. Important to remember that once a wrapper has a value assigned to it that value cannot be changed. Example:

```java
import java.util.*;
public class ABC{
    public static void main(String argv[]){
    Vector vct = new Vector();
    vct.add(new Integer(100));
    vct.add(new Integer(200));
    for(int i=0; i < vct.size();i ++){
        Integer in =(Integer) vct.get(i);
        System.out.println(in.intValue());
    }
    }
}
```

What are the different ways to handle exceptions?

Two ways to handle exceptions, a) Basic Try Catch Finally: Put desired code in a try block followed by a catch block to catch the exceptions, finally for garbage collection etc.
Example:

```java
public void Divide(){
        try {
              int res1 = div(200,100);
 int res2 = div(200,0);
           System.out.println(res);
        } catch (BadNumberException ex) {
            System.out.println(ex.getMessage());
        }
        System.out.println("Div done !");
    }

public void div(int Divide, int DivideBy)
    throws BadNumberException{
        if(DivideBy == 0){
            throw new BadNumberException("Cannot divide by Zero");
        }
        return Divide /DivideBy;
    }
```

b) Exception Hierarchies: List the desired exceptions in the throws clause of the method and let the caller of the method handle those exceptions.
Example:

```java
 public void method() throws IOException, FileNotFoundException{
//code
}
```

What are the execution criteria of finally block?

If try block is executed then finally block will automatically executes. If you write return as the last statement in the try block and no exception occurs, the finally block will still execute. After finally block execution only return statement executes. Fnally block will not execute when you say System.exit (0); the control immediately goes out of the program, and thus finally never executes.

What is garbage collection in Java?

Garbage collection will reclaim the memory, which is dynamically allocated that is no longer referenced. Because the heap is garbage-collected, Java programmers don't have to explicitly free allocated memory.
Example: System.gc(); You can explicitly reclaim the memory of a specific de-referenced object, invoking the garbage collector requires a simple two-step process.
a)create a Java Runtime object.
b)invoke the gc() method.
Example:

```java
Runtime g = Runtime.getRuntime();
g.gc();
```

What is finalize() ?
Finalization will be processed before the object is garbage collected.Each class inherits the finalize() method from java.lang.Object which is called by the garbage collector when it determines no more references are exist to the object . The finalize() method never run more than once on any object .The Object class finalize method performs no actions but it may be overridden by any class, Example:

```
protected void finalize() throws Throwable {
    try {
        // resource closing
    } finally {
        super.finalize();
    }
}
```

If any exception thrown by finalize() during garbage collection, it halts the finalization . Finalize can be used to release the resources like closing the file etc. What is Locale class? java.util.Locale object represents a specific geographical, political, or cultural region. Example:

```
Locale[] locs = Locale.getAvailableLocales();
    for(int j = 0; j < locs.length; j++){
      String lang = locs[j].getLanguage();
      String count = locs[j].getCountry();
      String locName = locs[j].getDisplayName();
      System.out.println(j + ": " + lang + ", " + count + ", " + locName);
    }
```

What is daemon thread?
A Daemon thread is low priority service provider thread, which runs intermittently in the back ground during runtime for garbage collection operation. setDaemon(boolean) : This method is used to set that a thread is daemon thread or not. public boolean isDaemon() : This method is used to check the thread is daemon thread or not. Example:

```
public class DaemThread extends Thread {}

public static void main(String[] args) {
 DaemThread thrd = new DaemThread();
 thrd .setDaemon(true);
 thrd .start();
}
```

What is JDBC (Java Database Connectivity) connection? How to achieve connection?

The JDBC is a Java API defines interfaces and classes for reading/writing database applications in Java by making database connections.
Steps to get connected DB,
a) Register the database driver:
Class.forName(specific DB driver class);
b) Create a database connection:
Connection conn = DriverManager.getConnection(url,username,password);
c) Create a query:
PreparedStatement stm= Conn.prepareStatement(SQL query);
d) Exceute the query :
stm.exceuteUpdate();

What method all threads must implement?

run(), whether it is a subclass of Thread or implement the Runnable interface.
```
Example:Extend Thread.
class ABCThread extends Thread {
    public ABCThread (String str) {
super(str);
    }
    public void run() {
            try {
//code
    } catch (InterruptedException e) {
}
    }
}
Example:Implement Runnable
class ABCRun implements Runnable{
char ch;
ABCRun(char c) {
    ch = c;
}
public void run() {
        try{
            //code
        } catch( InterruptedException e ) {
        }
}
}
```

What modifiers are allowed for methods and variables in an Interface?

Modifiers for variables in Interface: public, static and final Modifiers for methods in Interface: public and abstract
```
Example:
public interface ABC {
    public static final int val = 1;
    public abstract void mehtod(...);
}
```

What are types of modifier?

Access modifiers are used to set the visibility and accessibility of a class, its member variables, and methods. Access or Non-Access Control Modifiers Used for Description public class Accessible Anywhere or visible to the world.

Access or Non-Access Control Modifiers	Used for	Description
public	class	Accessible Anywhere or visible to the world.
public	interface	Accessible Anywhere or visible to the world.
public	member	Accessible anywhere wherever its class is.
private	member	Visible to the class only.
protected	member	Visible to the package and all its subclasses of any package.
abstract	class	Cannot be instantiated and this class contains unimplemented methods.
abstract	interface	All interfaces are by default abstract. Optional in declarations.
abstract	method	Methods without body, it has only signature. The enclosing class is abstract.
static	class	An inner class becomes top-level class.
static	method	Class methods invoked through the class name with dot operator.
static	field	Class fields invoked through the name of class.
static	initializer	It runs when the class is loaded, rather than when an instance is created.
final	class	Cannot be subclassed, finalizing the implementations.
final	method	Methods cannot be overridden and dynamically looked up.
final	field	Fields cannot change its value and these are compile-time constants.
final	variable	Cannot change final variables value.
synchronized	method	synchronized keyword is used preferably for methods where multithreading is implemented. For a static method, a lock is acquired before executing the method for the class. For a non-static method, a lock is acquired for the specific object instance.
transient	field	Cannot serialize with the object.
volatile	field	Accessed by unsynchronized threads.
native	method	Methods with no body, only signature, and platform-dependent.
none(package) or default modifier .	class	Accessible only within package.
none(package) or default modifier .	interface	Accessible only within package.
none(package) or default modifier .	member	Accessible only within package.
strictfp	class	In this class, all methods are implicitly strictfp.

strictfp	method	All floating-point operations done are strictly conforms to the IEEE 754 standard. All values should be expressed as IEEE float or double values.

What is a variable?
A variable is used to hold data that changes during the execution of the program.

What is scope of variable?

Scope of a variable means lifetime of a variable, where it defines the time for which the variable is existed in a program.
Example:
```
public class ABC {
  public static void main(String[] args) {
    int outerBlk = 100;

    {
      int innerBlk = 200;
      System.out.println("innerBlk = " + innerBlk);
      System.out.println("outerBlk = " + outerBlk);
    }

    int innerBlk = 300;
    System.out.println("innerBlk = " + innerBlk);
    System.out.println("outerBlk = " + outerBlk);
  }
}
Output:
outerBlk = 100
innerBlk = 300
outerBlk = 100
```

What are the different types of variable scopes?

The scope of a variable is determined by the context in which the variable is declared.
Types of Scopes,
a) Local variable: These variables are defined within a method. They remain accessible only during the course of execution of a method. When the method completes its execution, these variables fall out of scope.
b) Instance variable: Typically these are object level variables, they are initialized to default values at the time of object creation, and remain accessible as long as the object is existed/reachable.
c) Static variable: These variables are called class level variables because they are not tied to any particular object instance. They are initialized for the first time when the class is loaded in JVM and remain there as long as the class is reloaded.

What is the default value of the local variables?
Default value is not initialized to local variable, neither primitives nor object references. You need specify the value of variable explicitly; otherwise java compiler will not compile the code.

What is the scope of variable?
The block of code within which the variable is accessible defines the scope of a variable. The scope determines, a)When variable is created? b)When it possibly becomes a candidate for destruction?

What are primitive variable types?

Data Type	Bit Size	Usage	Signed	Range of Values
boolean	1	true or false	no	true or false
char	16	unicode character	no	0 to $2^{16} - 1$
byte	8	very small integer number	yes	$-2^7 to 2^7 - 1$
short	16	small integer number	yes	$-2^{15} to 2^{15} - 1$
int	32	integer number	yes	$-2^{31} to 2^{31} - 1$
long	64	large integer number	yes	$-2^{63} to 2^{63} - 1$
float	32	single precision decimal number	yes	$\pm 3.4e^{38} to \pm 1.4e^{-45}$
double	64	double precision decimal number	yes	$\pm 1.8e^{308} to \pm 4.9e^{-324}$

What are Control flow statements?

Control flow statements changes the flow of execution by performing decision-making, looping, and branching, that enabling your program to conditionally execute particular blocks of code. When a program makes a decision, it is determining, based on the state of the program data, whether certain lines of code should be executed. Control flow statements use to make decisions about which statements to execute and to otherwise change the flow of execution in a program. The bellow table shows the categories of control flow statements.

Category	Keyword	Purpose
Selection or Decision-Making Statements	if, if-else, switch	Execute a block or set of other statements only if certain conditions are met.
Loop Statements	while, do-while, for	This allows you to execute the set of statements to be repeated or looped through a fixed number of times.
Exception	throw, throws, try-catch, finally	Exception statements are normally used to handle unusual events or errors that arises while a program is running.

Branch Statements	continue, break, return	*continue* statements are used in looping statements to force another iteration of the loop before reaching the end of the current one. *break* statements are used in looping. *return* statements are used to force a quick exit from a method. They are also used to pass values back from methods. and *switch* statements to force an abrupt termination or exit from the loop or switch.

What is expression and when it is required?
An expression is a combination of variables, constants, operators, and method invocations, which are evaluated to a single value. The Expressions can have a single operation or multiple operations combined to form a compound expression.

When expression required?

a).To compute the values,
Example:45 +35*98-34;
b)To assign values to the variables, Example:
`int a=88,b=99;`
`int exp=a*b;`
c)To control the flow of execution. Example:
 	
`int a=55,b=68;`
`if(a*b >300)`
`{`
`//statements`
`}`
 	
Expressions are the basic components of statements and these statements are terminated by the semicolon character ';'.

Explain the working of Java Virtual Machine (JVM) in Java?
JVM is software that is responsible for running Java programs (runtime environment). JVM interprets the byte code (.class file which contains virtual machine instructions) to a machine dependent native code. The output of JVM (the native code) contains low-level instructions, which is easily understandable by the processors which process the native code to give the required output. JVM contains the following components: a.Class loader b.Byte code checker c.JIT compiler and interpreter

What is package?

It is a mechanism of organizing Java classes into namespaces. Java packages can be stored in JAR files (compressed files), allowing classes to download faster as a group rather than one at a time. Packages typically used to organize classes belonging to the same category or providing similar functionality and also provide a unique namespace for the types it contains. Classes in the same package can access each other's package members depending upon visibility.
Example:

```
package animals;
import behavior.*;
public class man {
  public static void main(String[] args) {
//code
  }
}
```

What is singleton class?

Only one object can be created at a time from a class called singleton class. This class contains a static method that returns its instance. A new singleton instance will be created when a singleton class is garbage -collected or reloaded.
Example:

```
public class ABCSingleton {
private static ABCSingleton inst = null;
protected ABCSingleton() {
}
public static ABCSingleton getinst() {
if(inst == null) {
inst = new ABCSingleton();
}
return inst;
}
}
```

List the disadvantages of Threads in Java.

a) There could be a deadlock issue, Race condition may arrive and starvation may happen.

b) Threads are totally Operating Systems dependent.

c) Global variables are shared between threads, hence there are chances of getting unexpected data.

d) Threads are executed serially (looks like parallel execution but actually it is serial execution) may increase the time complexity.

e) Many library functions are not thread safe; they are not a safer in the control flow.

f) The whole application crashes if any one of the threads crashes.

g) Unlike processes, memory crash in one thread kills other threads because of sharing the same memory.

What is a referent?

A 'final' keyword is used in the declaration for reference variables or constants; its value is immutable and cannot be modified to refer to any other object. Thus the 'final' specifier applies to the value of the variable itself, and not to the object referenced by the variable. Example:

```
  private final String Str=Hi;
```

Does java support Multiple Inheritance?

Multiple inheritance causes more problems and confusion than it solves. Directly this is not achievable, but indirectly can be done through implementing number of interfaces. In Java, you can extend only one class by other class.
Example:

```
import java.io.Serializable;
public class updateCell extends
Object implements Serializable {
}
```

What is List interface?

List interface is part of java.util package. List can implement Vector, ArrayList class. List value can get by Iterator interface. It is ordered collection of objects. List interface can add value elements by add(value) method.
Example:

```
import java.util.List;
import java.util.ArrayList;
import java.util.Iterator;
public class listTest {
    public static void main(String[] args) {
        List<String> lst=new ArrayList<String>();
        lst.add("val-1");
        lst.add("val-2");
        lst.add("val-3");

        Iterator iter=lst.iterator();
        while(iter.hasNext())
        {
          String val=(String)iter.next();
          System.out.println(val);
        }
    }
}
output:
val-1
val-2
val-3
```

Can we enforce garbage collection in java?

No, you cannot force Garbage Collection, but you can request for it by calling the method System.gc(). However it doesn't mean that Garbage Collection will start immediately. The GC is a low priority thread of JVM.

How can you call a constructor from another constructor and super class?

By using this () and super () respectively.
Example:
`public class Test1 {`
`public Test1() {`
`this("Test1"); //this function`
`}`
`public Test1(String arg) {`
`System.out.println(arg);`
`}`
`public static void main(String[] args) {`
`new Test1();`
`}`
`}`
`public class Test2 extends Test1{`
`    public Test2() {`
`        super(); //super function`
`    }`
`    public Test2(String arg) {`
`        System.out.println(arg);`
`    }`
`    public static void main(String[] args) {`
`new Test2();`
`}`
`}`
`output:`
`Test1`

What is de-serialization?

It is the process of restoring the state of an object. Deserialization is the inverse process of reconstructing an object from a byte stream to the same state in which the object was previously serialized.
Example:
`ObjectInputStream desObj = new ObjectInputStream(`
`new FileInputStream(new File(text.txt)));`
`System.out.println("The content : "+ desObj.readObject());`
`desObj.close();`

What is a native method?
It is a method and implemented in a language other than Java. e.g., C++ The Java native method is a way to gain and merge the solution of C or C++ programming into Java.

Which is the base class for all classes in Java?
java.lang.Object.

What is casting? How many types of casting?

It is the process of converting one type to another or changing an entity of one datatype into another. There are two types of casting.

a) Primitive type Casting: To convert larger data types to smaller data types.

Example: Convert from boolean to byte

```
boolean bl = true;
byte bt = 1;
bt = (byte)(bl?1:0);
```

b) Object references Casting: It is used to refer to an object by a compatible class, interface, or array type reference. With objects, you can cast an instance of a subclass to its parent class and it is called as upcasting.Downcasting is to cast from a base class to a more specific class. The cast does not convert the object, just asserts it actually is a more specific extended object.

Example:

```
class Animal {
int a = 123;
}
class Mammal extends Animal { }
class Cat extends Mammal { }
class Dog extends Mammal { }
public class TestUpcast {
 public static void main(String[] args) {
Cat cat = new Cat();
    System.out.println(cat.a);
    Mammal mam = cat; // upcasting here !
    System.out.println(mam.a);
 }
}
Output:
123
123
```

What is hashCode?

It is a is number (32-bit signed int) that allows an object to be managed by a hash-based data structure. A *hashcode* is treated as equivalent to object for fast compute based on all or most of the internal state of an object, use all or most of the space of 32-bit integers in a fairly uniform way , and likely to be different even for objects that are very similar. If you are overriding *hashCode* you need to override equals method also.
Example:

```
public class Test{
public static void main(String[] args){
String str1=new String("JAVA");
String str2=new String("KAVA");
String str3=new String("JAVA");

System.out.println("str1==str3:"+str1==str3);
System.out.println(str1.equals(str3));
System.out.println(str1.hashCode());
System.out.println(str3.hashCode());

System.out.println("str1==str2:"+str1==str2);
System.out.println(str1.equals(str2));
System.out.println(str1.hashCode());
System.out.println(str2.hashCode());
 }
}
Output:
false
true
2269730
2269730
false
false
2269730
2299521
```

What is class loader in java?

A class loader is one of the classes, it is responsible for loading the class. All JVM contains one class loader called primordial class loader. When a class is loaded, all classes its associated references are loaded too. The process of loading happens recursively, until all classes needed are loaded. It is not necessarily loading all classes in the application. Unreferenced classes are not loaded until the time they are referenced.
The steps followed by a class loader:
1. Check weather class was already loaded.
2. If not loaded, ask base class loader to load the class.
3. If base class loader cannot load a class, attempt to load it in this class loader.
Example:

```
public class Test {
        public static void main(String [] args) {
              try {
                    Class clz = Class.forName("java.util.HashSet");
  if (clz != null) {
                    Object obj = clz.newInstance();
  ((java.util.HashSet)obj).add("ONE");
  ((java.util.HashSet)obj).add("TWO");

java.util.Iterator it =  ((java.util.HashSet)obj).iterator();
while (it.hasNext()){
    System.out.println(it.next() );
  }
                  }
                  } catch (Exception e) {
                    System.err.println("Problem in loadind a class "
                    + "java.util.HashSet");
                  }
              }
        }
output:
TWO
ONE
```

What is JAR (Java Archive) file?

This is a file format that enables you to bundle multiple files into a single archive file. JAR files will contains a MANIFEST.MF file inside META-INF folder that describes the version and other features of jar file.

What is JIT (Just In Time compiler) ?

It compiles java byte code to native code or platform-specific executable code that is immediately executed. JIT compiler option should be used especially if the method executable is repeatedly reused in the code. The JIT compiler maintains a table called the V-table , it has two tables one for the addresses of the bytecode and another for the native code that is created using the bytecode.During the first time execution of a method, it is converted to the native code by the JIT compiler and address of the native code for that particular method is stored in the table. Then during subsequent execution the native is called for execution and this improves the speed of the execution.

What is internationalization?
Internationalization is the process of designing an application, so that it can be applicable to various languages and regions without changes.

What is volatile variable?
Volatile is used to indicate that a variable's value will be modified by different threads. a)The value of this variable will never be cached thread-locally: all reads and writes will go straight to "main memory"; b)Access to the variable acts as though it is enclosed in a synchronized block, synchronized on itself.

What is abstraction?
An abstraction is a concept , which make up the concrete events or things, which the abstraction refers to the referents.

What is encapsulation?

Encapsulation describes the ability of an object to hide its data and methods from the rest of the world. This technique involves, making the fields in a class private (it cannot be accessed by anyone outside the class) and providing access to the fields via public methods, this also referred to as data hiding. Access to the data and code is tightly controlled by an interface. The main advantage of encapsulation is the ability to modify our implemented code without breaking the code of others who use our code. With this feature Encapsulation gives maintainability, flexibility and extensibility to our code. Example:
 	
``java
 public class Test{
    private String name;
     public void setName(String nm){
       name = nm;
 }
public String getName(){
     return name;
 }
 public static void main(String args[]){
       Test t = new Test();
       t.setName("Chandru");
       System.out.print("Name: " + t.getName());
    }
}
Output:
Name: Chandru
``

What is inheritance?
Inheritance is the ability to create new classes based on existing classes or capability of a class to use the properties and methods of another class while adding its own functionality. It is useful to reuse existing code. This defines is-a relationship between a superclass and its subclasses. Inheritance is not possible in below cases, 1. A subclass can extend only one superclass at a time. 2. Private members of the superclass are not inherited by the subclass and can only be indirectly accessed by setters and getters of public methods. 3. Since constructors and initializer blocks are not members of a class, they are not inherited by a subclass. 4. Members that have default accessibility in the superclass are also not inherited by subclasses in other packages, as these members are only accessible by their simple names in subclasses within the same package as the superclass.

How state and behavior is associated to objects?
OOPs objects are conceptually similar to real-time objects, which consist of state and related behavior expressed through the members of class. In real programming, an object stores its state in fields and its behavior in methods. Example: A bird can have state like name, and its behavior like flying.

What is a Socket? What are advantages and disadvantages?
A socket is a link between two programs running on the network to achieve two-way communication. Socket classes are used to represent the connection between a client program and a server program. The java.net package has two classes, Socket: implement the client side of the connection ServerSocket: implement the server side of the connection Advantages of Java Sockets: a)Sockets are flexible and sufficient. b)Efficient for general communications. c)Sockets cause low network traffic. Disadvantages of Java Sockets: a)Security restrictions. b)Socket based communications allows only to send packets of raw data between applications.

List the primitive types and the corresponding wrapper classes.

a)void - java.lang.Void
b)Primitive Wrapper
c)boolean - java.lang.Boolean
d)byte - java.lang.Byte
e)char - java.lang.Character
f)float - java.lang.Float
g)double - java.lang.Double
h)int - java.lang.Integer
i)long - java.lang.Long
j)short - java.lang.Short

Does a class inherit the constructors of its base (super) class?

A class does not inherit constructors from any of its base class.

What is the use of System class?

System class is to provide access to system resources.

When explicit object casting is needed? Give example for the same.

You need to do explicit casting when you assign a superclass object to a variable of a subclass's data type.
Example: Vehicle is super class and Car is subclass.
Vehicle v;
Car c;
c = (Car) v;

What is the order of catch statements for super class and subclass?

Exception of subclasses has to be caught first.

What is Object class in Java?

The Object class is a superclass for all user-defined Java classes and Javas class libraries. A Java object is an instance of any class which is derived from the Object class. Usually, when a class is defined in Java, implicitly the Object class is inherited.
Example:
public class ABC is same as public class ABC extends Object

If some important event has happened in one class, how to inform this action to other class?

If you are using regular classes, use the Observer interface. If these classes are implements/exteds Runnable/Thread classes, then consider *notify () or notifyAll()*.

What are the different levels of locking by using synchronization?

```
1) Block level lock
Example:  synchronized (this) {//code}
2) Method level lock
Example:  public synchronized void method() {           //code     }
3)  Object level lock
Example:  private Object lock = new Object();
synchronized(lock) {
          //code
   }
4) Class level lock
Example: class Test {
    static synchronized public method() {
       //code
    }
}
```

What is the use of prepared statement in Java?

PreparedStatement is derived from the more general class Statement. PreparedStatement are precompiled statements, generally used in bulk processing to speed up the process of inserting, updating and deleting.
Example:
```
      Class.forName("com.mysql.jdbc.Driver");
      Connection con = DriverManager.getConnection
      ("jdbc:mysql://localhost:3306/jdbctutorial","root","root");
      PreparedStatement prest = con.prepareStatement
      ("UPDATE EMPLOYEES SET SALARY = 10000  ");
      ResultSet rs = prest.executeQuery();
```

What is callable statement?
It is used to invoke the stored procedures. You can obtain the callablestatement from Connection using the methods *prepareCall*(String sql) and *prepareCall*(String sql, int resultSetType, int resultSetConcurrency)

What is Annotations in Java?

Annotations in Java are used to add the meta-data facility to the Java Elements. It is a data about a program that is not part of the program and has no impact on the operation of the code they annotate. Annotations can be applied to program declarations of classes, fields, methods, and other program elements.
Annotations used as,
a)Information for the compiler: The compiler to detect errors or suppress warnings can use Annotations.
b)Compiler-time processing: Software tools can process annotation information to generate code, etc.
c)Deployment-time processing: Software tools can process annotation information to generate XML files, etc
d)Runtime processing: annotations are available at runtime.
Example:
`@Tree (`
`    Name = "Mango",`
`    Age = "23"`
`)`
`class ABC() { }`

What is Auto boxing?
Autoboxing is a new feature in Java 5, Java compiler makes automatic conversion between the primitive (basic) types and their corresponding object wrapper classes (eg, int to Integer, double to Double, etc). Example: int num=10; Intager numObj =num;

What is Auto unboxing?
In Auto unboxing, wrapper types are automatically converted into their primitive equivalents if needed for assignments or method or constructor invocations. Example: int num = 0; num = new Integer(10);

Why we should prefer primitive data types rather than Object wrapper classes?
Primitive data types faster than the corresponding wrapper types, and immutability (can't be changed after creation) of the wrapper types .

What is Scanners?
java.util.Scanner is a new feature in Java 5,it is used to read values from System.in or a file. A simple text scanner which can parse primitive types and strings using regular expressions. Basically,a Scanner breaks its input value into tokens using a delimiter pattern(by default matches whitespace). The resulting tokens may then be converted into values of different types using the various next (nextInt, nextLong, etc) methods. Example: Scanner scan = new Scanner(System.in); int num = scan.nextInt();

What is instanceof operator?
It is a type comparison operator, determine if an object belongs to a specific class, or implements a specific interface. It returns true if an object is an instance of the class or if the object implements the interface, otherwise it returns false. Example:

```
public class Test {
            public static void main(String[] args){
String str1 = "abc";
String str2 = null;
if(str1 instanceof java.lang.String)
System.out.println("str1:It is a String object !");
else
System.out.println("str1:It is not a String object !");

if(str2 instanceof java.lang.String)
System.out.println("str2:It is a String object !");
else
System.out.println("str2:It is not a String object !");
    }
}
Output:
str1:It is a String object !
str2:It is not a String object !
```

What is literal?

A literal is the representation of a fixed/physical value; literals are represented directly in the code without requiring computation.
Example:
```
char c = 'C';
boolean bl = false;
int i = 3;
byte bt = 2;
```

How to copy arrays in JAVA?

In Java, System class has an arraycopy method (built in method) that can be used to copy elements from one array into another efficiently: Method: public static void arraycopy(Object source, int source_position,Object destination, int destination_position, int length)
Here,
Object source: specifies the source array name.
Object destination: specifies the destination array name.
int source_position : starting position in the source array
int destination_position: starting position in the destination array
int length :the number of array elements to copy.
Example:
```
class Test {
    public static void main(String[] args) {
        char[] src = { '1', '2', '3', '4', '5', '6', '7' };
        char[] dest = new char[10];
System.out.println("Before copy:"+new String(dest));
        System.arraycopy(src, 3, dest, 0, 3);
        System.out.println("After copy:"+new String(dest));
    }
}
Output:
Before copy:
After copy:456
```

What are Branching Statements?

break, continue and return.

What is nested classes?

It is the process of defining a class within another class. A nested class is a member of its enclosing class. Nested is a logical grouping of classes that are only used in one place can lead to more readable and maintainable code with encapsulation.

Two types of nested classes,

a) Static nested classes

b) Non Static nested classes (inner classes)

Static nested classes:

It is associated with its outer class, cannot refer directly to instance variables or methods defined in its enclosing class , it can use them only through an object reference.

Example:

```java
class Outer {
    class Inner
    {
      public  void innerMethod() {
            System.out.println("innerMethod");
      }
    }
 public  void outerMethod() {
            System.out.println("outerMethod");
    }
}
public class Test {
    public static void main(String[] args) {
            Outer outobj=new Outer();
            Outer.Inner innerobj=outobj.new  Inner();
outobj.outerMethod();
innerobj.innerMethod();
    }
}
```

Output:

outerMethod

innerMethod

Non Static nested classes (inner classes): inner class is associated with an instance of its enclosing class and has direct access to that object's methods and fields, it cannot define any static members itself.

Example:

```java
class Outer {
  static  class Inner
    {
      public  void innerMethod() {
            System.out.println("innerMethod");
      }
    }
 public  void outerMethod() {
            System.out.println("outerMethod");
    }
}
public class Test {
    public static void main(String[] args) {
            Outer outobj=new Outer();
            Outer.Inner innerobj=new Outer.Inner();
outobj.outerMethod();
innerobj.innerMethod();
    }
}
```

Output:

outerMethod

innerMethod

Rules : a) You cannot create a static member inside the nested class.

b) Nested class can be declared abstract or final.

c) If you have a static nested class, you cannot access the methods and variables of the outer class from the static nested (inner) class.

d) To have instance of nested class you must have a instance of outer class.

What is Enum Type?

enum type is a type whose fields consist of a fixed set of constants. enum instances describe values, where the set of possible values are finite. Enumerated type is used when the most important information is the existence of the value. All enums implicitly extend java.lang.Enum.
Example:

```
enum Day {
    SUNDAY, MONDAY, TUESDAY, WEDNESDAY,THURSDAY, FRIDAY, SATURDAY
}
public class Test {
    public static void main(String args[])
    {
        Day d = Day.THURSDAY;
        switch(d) {
            case SUNDAY:
                System.out.println("Day-7");
                break;
            case MONDAY:
                System.out.println("Day-1");
                break;
            case TUESDAY:
                System.out.println("Day-2");
                break;
            case WEDNESDAY:
                System.out.println("Day-3");
                break;
case THURSDAY:
                System.out.println("Day-4");
                break;
            case FRIDAY:
                System.out.println("Day-5");
                break;
            case SATURDAY:
                System.out.println("Day-6");
                break;
            default:
                System.out.println("Invalid day !");
                break;
        }
    }
}
Output:
Day-4
```

What are the methods inherited from Object superclass?

Every class inherits the instance methods of Object.

i.protected Object clone() throws *CloneNotSupportedException*

Creates and returns a copy of this object.

ii.public boolean equals(Object obj)

Indicates whether some other object is "equal to" this one.

iii.protected void finalize() throws Throwable

Called by the garbage collector on an object when garbage collection determines that there are no more references to the object

iv.public final Class getClass()

Returns the runtime class of an object.

v.public int hashCode()

Returns a hash code value for the object.

vi.public String toString()

Returns a string representation of the object.

vii.public final void notify()

wakes up the first thread that called wait( ) on the same object.

viii.public final void notifyAll()

wakes up all the threads that called wait( ) on the same object. The highest priority thread will run first.

ix.public final void wait()

Causes current thread to wait until another thread invokes the *notify()* method or the *notifyAll()* method for this object.

x.public final void wait(long timeout)

Causes current thread to wait until either another thread invokes the *notify()* method or the *notifyAll()* method for this object, or a specified amount of time has elapsed.

xi. public final void wait(long timeout, int nanos) Causes current thread to wait until another thread invokes the *notify()* method or the *notifyAll()* method for this object, or some other thread interrupts the current thread, or a certain amount of real time has elapsed.

What is bounded type parameters?

A type parameter with one or more bounds. The bounds restrict the set of types that can be used as type arguments and give access to the methods defined by the bounds.
Example:

```java
public class Test
{
    public static <S extends Comparable<S>> S max(S a, S b, S c)
    {
        S max = a;
        if ( b.compareTo( max ) > 0 ){
            max = b;
        }
        if ( c.compareTo( max ) > 0 ){
            max = c;
        }
        return max;
    }
    public static void main( String args[] )
    {
System.out.println( "max is:"+max( 11, 22, 1 ) );
System.out.println( "max is:"+max( 1.1, 2.2, 0.5 ) );
System.out.println( "max is:"+max( "B", "A", "D"  ) );
    }
}
Output:
max is:22
max is:2.2
max is:D
```

What is Constructor?

a)Constructors are used to initialize the instance variables of an object.

b)Constructors are similar to methods, during creation of a new instance (a new object) of a class using the new keyword, a constructor for that class is called.

c)Default constructor is created only if there are no constructors. They do not have return types.

d)The first line of a constructor must either be a call on another constructor in the same class (this), or a call on the superclass constructor (using super).

e)Constructor cannot be inherited. Example:

```
 public class Test
{
   private int v;
   public Test(){
       System.out.println("Hi");
   }
   public Test(int val){
v=val;
   }

   public static void main( String args[] )
   {
Test t= new Test();
Test t1= new Test(100);
System.out.println(t1.v);
   }
}
Output:Hi
100
```

Types of Object Creation techniques in JAVA?

a) By using new keyword:

Example:Test obj = new Test();

b) By using Class.forName():

Example:Test obj= (Test) Class.forName(com.abc.Test).newInstance();

c) By using clone():

Example:Test obj= new Test(); Test obj1= obj.clone();

d) By using object deserialization technique

Example: ObjectInputStream obj =new ObjectInputStream(inputStream);

Test obj1 = (Test) obj.readObject();

e) By using class loader:

Example:this.getClass().getClassLoader().loadClass(com.abc.Test).newInstance();

What is final modifier?

The final modifier keyword makes that , value cannot be changed anymore.

a) final Classes: A final class cannot have be sub classed.

b) final Variables: A final variable cannot be altered once it is initialized.

c) final Methods: A final method cannot be overridden by subclasses.

What is the use of static block?

Static block will be executed exactly once when the class is first loaded into JVM. Before accessing the main method the static block will be executed. Example:
 	
``java
public class Test{
    static{
        //some statements here
    }
}
``

What is the *Set* interface ?
The *Set* interface provides methods for accessing the elements of a finite mathematical set without duplicate elements. It contains all methods which is implementations of the List interface are, i. HashSet ii. TreeSet iii.LinkedHashSet iv. EnumSet

What is a HashSet ?

A HashSet is an unsorted, unordered Set. It uses the hashcode of the object being inserted. Duplicates are not allowed. Example:
 	
``java
import java.util.*;
public class Test {
  public static void main(String [] args) {
    int size;
    HashSet <String>hSet = new HashSet <String>();
    String str1 = "A", str2 = "Z";
    Iterator iterator;
 	
    hSet.add(str1);
    hSet.add(str2);
 	
    System.out.print("Values : ");
    iterator = hSet.iterator();
    while (iterator.hasNext()){
      System.out.print(iterator.next() + " ");
    }
 	
  }
}
Output: Values: Z A
``

What is a TreeSet ?

This keeps the elements in sorted order. The elements are sorted according to the natural order of elements or by the comparator provided at creation time.
Example:

```java
import java.util.*;
public class Test{
  public static void main(String[] args) {
    TreeSet <Integer>tree = new TreeSet<Integer>();
    tree.add(123);
    tree.add(345);
    tree.add(12);
    System.out.print("Tree before deletion: ");
    Iterator iterator;
    iterator = tree.iterator();
    while (iterator.hasNext()){
      System.out.println(iterator.next() );
    }
     System.out.println("");
    if (tree.remove(12)){
      System.out.println("12 is deleted");
    }
    else{
      System.out.println("12 doesn't exist!");
    }
    System.out.print("Tree after deletion: ");
    iterator = tree.iterator();
    while (iterator.hasNext()){
      System.out.println(iterator.next() );
    }

  }
}
Output: Tree before deletion: 12
123
345
12 is deleted
Tree after deletion: 123
345
```

What is a Map?

a)A map stores pairs of key and value with associations between keys and values
b)Both keys and values are objects.
c)By a key, you can find its value.
d)The keys must be unique, but the values may be duplicated.
e)Maps can accept a null key and null values.
f)For inserting, deleting, and locating elements in a *Map*, the *HashMap* offers the best performance. Implementations of the List interface are,
i. HashMap
ii. HashTable
iii.TreeMap
iv. EnumMap

What is the Comparable interface?

The objects of the class implementing the Comparable interface can be ordered. The *Comparable* interface is used to sort collections and arrays of objects using the *Collections.sort()* and *java.utils.Arrays.sort()* methods respectively. All classes implementing the Comparable interface must implement the *compareTo()* method that has the return type as an integer.
The Comparable interface in the generic format,
interface Comparable¡S¿
where S is the name of the type parameter.
Example:

```java
import java.util.Comparator;
public class Test implements Comparator{
public int compare(Object valS, Object valT){
String NameS = ( (Test1) valS ).getName();
String NameT = ( (Test1) valT ).getName();
return NameS.compareTo(NameT);
}
}
```

What is a *TreeMap* ?

In a *TreeMap* the data will be sorted in ascending order of keys according to the natural order for the key's class, or by the comparator provided at creation time. *TreeMap* is based on the Red-Black tree data structure. *TreeMap* implements the *SortedMap* interface which extends the Map interface. *TreeMap* is your better solution when you need to traverse the keys in a sorted order.
Example:

```java
import java.util.*;
class Test {
public static void main(String args[]) {
TreeMap tMap = new TreeMap();
tMap.put("Vinod", new Double(22));
tMap.put("Shankar", new Double(44));
tMap.put("Kiran", new Double(11));
tMap.put("Chandru", new Double(1));

Set set = tMap.entrySet();
Iterator i = set.iterator();

while(i.hasNext()) {
Map.Entry map = (Map.Entry)i.next();
System.out.print(map.getKey() + ": ");
System.out.println(map.getValue());
}
}
}
Output:
Chandru: 1.0
Kiran: 11.0
Shankar: 44.0
Vinod: 22.0
```

What is Default constructor?

It is a constructor, which is automatically created by the compiler without parameters (default). The default constructor calls the default base (parent) constructor (super()) and initializes all instance variables to default value (zero/null/false for numeric types, object references, and Booleans respectively). This constructor does not perform any actions or initializations.
Example:
Test t = new Test ();

Why is the Java *main()* method static?

The JVM interpreter will call the program's public main method to start the program without creating an instance of the class (because it is static,), and the program does not return data to the JVM interpreter when it ends. main method is part of its class and not part of objects. When can an object reference be cast to an interface reference? An object reference is cast to an interface reference as soon as the object implements the referenced interface. Which class do all other classes extend? Object class

---

Is JAVA multi-level inheritance or multiple inheritances?

JAVA supports multi-level inheritance.

What is MVC Architecture?

MVC stands for Model View Controller, a Model can include bean, EJB; View can include Html, JSP and finally Controller can include Servlet.MVC pattern or architecture is a sequence of action interactions starting with view, then controller and then to model based on the data persistence. Model is responsible for holding the application state, View is for displaying the current model and controller handles the event.

What is runtime polymorphism?

Polymorphism allows you to define one interface and have multiple implementations e.g., method overriding. A method in subclass overrides the method in its super classes with the same name and signature. Runtime polymorphism is also called as dynamic method dispatch. At runtime, which version of the method will be invoked is based on the type of actual object stored in that reference variable and not on the type of the reference variable. Example:

```java
class T {
  void method() {
    System.out.println("I am a T.");
  }
}
class T1 extends T {
  void method() {
    System.out.println("I am a T1.");
  }
}
class T2 extends T {
  void method() {
    System.out.println("I am a T2.");
  }
}
class T3 extends T {
  void method() {
    System.out.println("I am a T3.");
  }
}

class Test {

  public static void main(String[] args) {
    T ref1 = new T();
    T ref2 = new T1();
    T ref3 = new T2();
    T ref4 = new T3();
    ref1.method();
    ref2.method();
    ref3.method();
    ref4.method();
  }
}
```
Output:
I am a T.
I am a T1.
I am a T2.
I am a T3.

What is property (.properties) file in JAVA?

The .properties is a file extension for files to store the configurable parameters of an application hence they are called as Property Resource Bundles. They can also be used for storing strings for Internationalization and localization. Each line in a .properties file normally stores a single property and each parameter in properties file is stored as a pair of strings, one is storing key (name of the parameter), and the other is storing the value.
Some Example for formats:
a)key=value
b)key = value
c)key:value
d)key value
#or! is used to denote a comment in properties file and the backwards slash is used to escape a character.
Example:

```
Content of TestProperty.properties file
Test=This is a Test
Test1=This is a Test1

Content of  Test.java file
 import java.io.FileNotFoundException;
 import java.io.FileReader;
 import java.io.IOException;
 import java.util.Properties;

 public class Test {

     public static void main(String[] args) {
         Test test = new Test();
         test.readProperties();
     }

     public void readProperties(){
         FileReader filerdr = null;
         try{
             Properties prps = new Properties();
             filerdr = new FileReader("C:\\TestProperty.properties");
             prps.load(filerdr);
             System.out.println("Properties: " + prps.toString());
         }catch(FileNotFoundException exe){
             exe.printStackTrace();
         }catch(IOException ioe){
             ioe.printStackTrace();
         }finally{
             try{
                 filerdr.close();
             }catch(IOException e){
                 e.printStackTrace();
             }
         }
     }
 }

Output:
Properties: {Test1=This is a Test1, Test=This is a Test}
```

What is reflection?

It is used to inspect and dynamically call classes, methods, attributes, etc. at runtime. If you have an object of an unknown type in Java, and you would like to call a *'getValue'* method on it if that method is existed (you can confirm if interface existed) but using reflection, your code can look at the object and find out if it has a method called *'getValue'*, and then, call it if you required to call.

Example: Test test = HelloObj.getClass().getTest("getValue", null);

test.invoke(HelloObj, null);

How to execute PL-SQL is in JAVA?

Calling a PL/SQL Function from a JDBC application involves following steps,
1)Write a PL-SQL statements in a a String.
2) Create and prepare a JDBC *CallableStatement*(similar to the *PreparedStatement*) object that contains a call to your PL/SQL function.
3) Register the output parameter for your PL/SQL function.
4) Provide all of the required parameter values to your PL/SQL function.
5) Call the execute() method for your *CallableStatement* object, which then performs the call to your PL/SQL procedure.
6) Read the returned value from your PL/SQL function.
Example:

```
  public  static int count(Connection conn) {
  int count=0;
// query
  StringBuffer plSQL = new StringBuffer();
  plSQL.append("CREATE OR REPLACE FUNCTION counting RETURN number is " +
  "Name varchar(200); " +
  "cnt NUMBER := 0;   " +
  "CURSOR Cursor IS    SELECT name from TABLE ; " +
"BEGIN "+
"OPEN Cursor; " +
"LOOP " +
 " FETCH Cursor INTO Name; " +
  "EXIT WHEN Cursor%NOTFOUND;    " +
  "cnt := cnt +1; " +
"END LOOP; " +
"CLOSE Cursor; " +
"return(cnt); " +
"END;" );

  java.sql.Statement st=null;
  CallableStatement cs=null;
  try{
  st=conn.createStatement();
  st.execute(plSQL.toString());
  cs=conn.prepareCall("{?=call versionValidation}");
  cs.registerOutParameter(1,Types.INTEGER);
  cs.execute();
  count= cs.getInt(1);

  }catch(Exception exe){
  try{
  exe.printStackTrace();
  st.close();
  cs.close();
  }catch(Exception e){}
  return count;
  }
  return count;
  }
```

What happens when you invoke a thread's interrupt method while it is sleeping or waiting?
In this case task enters into the ready state.

What is the purpose of the File class?
The object of File class is used to access to the files and directories of a local file system.

How to read attributes/columns of Database tables through JDBC(JAVA)?
| ```
select COLUMN_NAME from USER_TAB_COLUMNS where TABLE_NAME='TABLE_NAME'
order by column_id;
This query will list out all column names existed in the TABLE_NAME.
USER_TAB_COLUMNS is having many attributes like DATA_TYPE, DATA_LENGTH,
NULLABLE etc.
``` |

What is JDBC connection pool?
JDBC connection pool is nothing but the way of storing established connections in the memory or pool all the connections at one place. JDBC connection pool is important when your application is tasked with servicing many concurrent users within the requirements of sub second response time. Once that particular database task is completed the connection is returned back to the pool. Every time a database connection needs to be established a request is made to pool or any object, which holds all the connections to provide a connection. What happens when a thread cannot acquire a lock on an object? It enters the waiting state until the lock becomes available.

Can an unreachable object become reachable again?
Yes. It can happen when the object's finalize() method is invoked and the object performs an process which causes it to become accessible to reachable objects.

What classes of exceptions may be caught by a catch clause?
It can catch any exception that may be assigned to the Throwable type including Error and Exception types. What happens if an exception is not caught in a program? An uncaught exception will invoke *uncaughtException()* method of the thread's ThreadGroup, which eventually results in the killing of the program in which it is thrown.

Which arithmetic operations can result in the throwing of an ArithmeticException?
and %
```

What is the use of a statement block?
A statement block is used to organize a succession of statements as a solitary statement group.

Can you call one constructor from another if a class has multiple constructors?

```
Yes, this is possible by using this().
Example:
public class Test {
 int x=10;
 Test(){
 this(2);
 }
 Test(int x){this.x=x;}

 public static void main(String args[])
 {
 Test t=new Test();
  System.out.println("value ="+t.x);
 }
}
Output:value=2
```

How would you make a copy of an entire Java object with its state?
By implementing a Cloneable interface and call its method clone ().

What interface must be implemented before it can be written to a stream as an object?
Serializable or *Externalizable* interface.

What is meant by StreamTokenizer?
StreamTokenizer splits up *InputStream* into tokens that are delimited by sets of characters.

What is a Stream?

A Stream is an abstraction that either constructs or consumes information. There are two stream types, they are: Byte Streams: handles bytes of input and output stream. Character Streams: handles character of input and output stream.

What is meant by time slicing or time-sharing?

This is the method of distributing CPU time to individual threads in a priority schedule.

Which method is used to find the class of an Object?

Use *getClass()* method on given Object , it will find out what class it belongs to. This method is defined in the object class and is available to all objects.

Why you want to call super explicitly?

If you want to invoke a parent constructor, which has parameters, at that time super needs to use explicitly.

Features

Features

17.3 PHP FAQS

What is PHP?

PHP(Hyper text Pre Processor) is a scripting language basically used for web applications, this language is more flexible than any other languages. Helps web developers to write dynamically generated pages quickly.
PHP is an HTML-embedded scripting language, its most of the syntaxes are borrowed from C, Java and Perl with a couple of unique PHP-specific features.

What is *include()* and *require()*?
We can include a file using *"include()"* or *"require()"* function with as its parameter. In *include()*, if the file is not found then a warning will be issued, but execution will continue. In case of *require()*, if the file is not found then it will cause a fatal error and halt the execution of the script. *require()* includes and evaluates a specific file, while *require_once()* does that only if it has not been included before.

What is the difference between mysql_fetch_object and mysql_fetch_array?
MySQL fetch object will collect first single matching record via mysql_fetch_object where as mysql_fetch_array will collect all matching records from the table in an array.

How do you define a constant?
Using *define*() directive, e.g., define ("CONST1",1000)

What is cookie in PHP?
A cookie is used for identification purposes like identifying a user in a session. It is a small file the application inserts on the users computer. PHP can create and retrieve the cookie.

What is a session?
Session is commonly used to store temporary data to allow multiple PHP pages to offer a complete functional transaction for the same visitor. It is a logical object created by the PHP engine to allow you to preserve data across subsequent HTTP requests. At any time, there is only one session object available to your PHP scripts, so data saved to the session by a script can be retrieved by the same script or another script when requested from the same visitor.

What is the use of the function *explode()*?
This function is used to divide/split a string by special character or symbol or delimiter in the string, we should pass the string and splitting character as parameter into the function.

What is meant by PEAR ?
PEAR is PHP Extension and Application Repository, it is a framework and distribution system for reusable PHP components. This repository is bringing higher level programming to PHP. It eases installation by bringing an automated wizard, and packing the strength and experience of PHP users into a nicely organised OOP library. PEAR also provides a command-line interface that can be used to automatically install "packages". The PEAR gives a structured library of open-sourced code for PHP users, a system for code distribution and package maintenance, a standard style for code written in PHP, PHP Foundation Classes (PFC), PHP Extension Community Library (PECL), web site, mailing lists and download mirrors to support the PHP/PEAR community, this implementation is still going on.

What is the difference between $message and $$message?
Both are variables, $message is a variable with a fixed name and $$message is a variable who's name is stored in $message. Example: if $message contains "var", $$message is the same as $var.

What is the difference between *echo* and *print* statement?
echo can accept multiple expressions while *print* cannot. *echo* is faster than print since it does not return a value where as *print* returns 1 or 0 depending on the success.

What is *zend* engine?
Zend Engine is used internally by PHP as a complier and runtime engine. PHP Scripts are loaded into memory and compiled into Zend opcodes, these opcodes are executed and the generated HTML code is sent to the client.

What is a Persistent Cookie?

In the PHP, by default cookies are created as temporary cookies which stored only in the browser's memory. When the browser is closed, temporary cookies will be deleted. A persistent cookie is permanent cookie which is stored in a cookie file permanently on the browser's computer. You should decide when to use temporary cookies and when to use persistent cookies based on their requirement:
a)Temporary cookies can not be used for tracking long-term information.
b)Persistent cookies can be used for tracking long-term information.
c)Temporary cookies are safer because no programs other than the browser can access them.
d)Persistent cookies are less secure because users can open cookie files see the cookie values.

What is CAPTCHA?

CAPTCHA is a test to determine if the user using the system is a human via web sites by asking code to users. Depending on the responses the identification can be made. *CAPTCHA* Creator is a PHP Script that generates Strong CAPTCHAS.

What is use of in_array() function in php ?

It is used to checks if a value exists in an array.

What is difference between developing website using Java and PHP?

For designing interactive pages, Java uses JSP (Java Server pages). PHP is an open source software while JSP is not. Libraries are much stronger in Java as compared to PHP. Huge codes can be managed with ease in Java by making classes, where as PHP team is still enhancing the features of PHP.

How to retrieve the data from MySQL result set ?

```
Use mysql_fetch_row, mysql_fetch_array, mysql_fetch_object,
 mysql_fetch_assoc.
```

What is meant by *urlencode* and *urldecode*?

urlencode() returns the URL encoded version of the given string. URL coding converts special characters into % signs followed by two hex digits.
Example: urlencode("20.00%") will return "20%2E00%25". URL encoded strings are safe to be used as part of URLs.
urldecode() returns the URL decoded version of the given string.
urlencode(str) returns the URL encoded version of the input string. String values to be used in URL query string need to be URL encoded. In the URL encoded version: Alphanumeric characters are maintained as is. Space characters are converted to "+" characters. Other non-alphanumeric characters are converted "%" followed by two hex digits representing the converted character.
urldecode(str) returns the original string of the input URL encoded string.
Example:
$discount ="20.00$url =
"http://domainname.com/submit.php?disc=".urlencode($discount); echo $url; You will get "http://domainname.com/submit.php?disc=20%2E00%25".

What is the difference between the functions *unlink* and *unset*?

Unlink is a function for file system handling which deletes a file. *Unset* is used to destroy a variable.

What is *Joomla* in PHP?

Joomla is an open source content management system, it can be used in PHP as a framework to publish web contents. It also allows the user to manage the content of the web pages with ease.

What is STRSTR() and STRISTR functions?

Both are used to find the first occurrence of a string. Both functions are used to return or finds the first occurrence of a substring from a string, and give all string from first occurrence to end of string except than *STRISTR()* is case-insensitive. If no match is found then FALSE will be returned.

What is meant by nl2br()?

Nl2br inserts HTML line breaks before all newlines in a string. nl2br("A B
C") will output "A B
C" to your browser.

What is the difference between Notify URL and Return URL?
Notify URL and Return URL is used in Paypal Payment Gateway integration. Notify URL is used by PayPal to post information about the transaction and Return URL is used by the browser; A url where the user needs to be redirected on completion of the payment process.

How can we encrypt the username and password using php?

```
It can encrypt a password with  Mysql>SET
PASSWORD=PASSWORD("Password");
We can encode data using base64_encode($str) and can decode
 using base64_decode($str);
```

What are the various methods to pass data from one web page to another web page?
1. Store the data in a session variable. By storing the data, the data can be passed from one page to another. 2. Store data in a cookie: By storing data in a persistent cookie, data can be passed from one form to another. 3. Set the data in a hidden field and post the data using a submit button.

What is SSL ?
SSL(Secure Sockets Layer) is a cryptographic protocols which provide secure communications on the Internet.

How can we send a mail ?

You cannot send emails directly using JavaScript. But you can use JavaScript to execute a client side email program and send the email using the "mailto" code.
Example:
`function myfunction(form)`
`{`
`tdata=document.myform.tbox1.value;`
`location="mailto:mailid@domain.com?subject=...";`
`return true;`
`}`

How to upload files using PHP?

Files can be uploaded in PHP by using the tag type=file. An upload form must have encytype="multipart/form-data" , method also needs to be set to method="post". Also, hidden input MAX_FILE_SIZE before the file input to restrict the size of files.
Example:
```
<form enctype="multipart/form-data" action="test.php"
method="POST">
<input type="hidden" name="MAX_FILE_SIZE" value="1000" />
```

How to add array elements?

"array_sum" method used for calculate sum of values in an array.

What is the use of "ksort"?

It is used for sort an array using key in reverse order.

What are the different types of errors in php?

```
E_ERROR: A fatal error that causes script termination
E_WARNING: Run-time warning that does not cause script termination
E_PARSE: Compile time parse error.
E_NOTICE: Run time notice caused due to error in code
E_CORE_ERROR: Fatal errors that occur during PHP's initial startup
(installation)
E_CORE_WARNING: Warnings that occur during PHP's initial startup
E_COMPILE_ERROR: Fatal compile-time errors indication problem with script.
E_USER_ERROR: User-generated error message.
E_USER_WARNING: User-generated warning message.
E_USER_NOTICE: User-generated notice message.
E_STRICT: Run-time notices.
E_RECOVERABLE_ERROR: Catchable fatal error indicating a dangerous error
E_ALL: Catches all errors and warnings
```

How do you create sub domains?

Wild card domains can be used. Sub domains can be created by first creating a sub directory in the /htdocs folder. E.g. /htdocs/mydomain. Then, the host file needs to be modified to define the sub domain. If the sub domains are not configured explicitly, all requests should be thrown to the main domain.

What is the difference between ereg_replace() and eregi_replace()?

eregi_replace() function is identical to *ereg_replace()* except that it ignores case distinction when matching alphabetic characters.

How to find out the number of parameters passed into a function ?
func_num_args() function returns the number of parameters passed in.

What is *Type Juggle*?

Type Juggling means dealing with a variable type. A variables type is determined by the context in which it is used. If an integer value is assigned to a variable, it becomes an integer.
Example:
`$var3= $var1 + $var2`
`Here, if $var1 is an integer. $var2 and $var3 will also be treated as integers.`

What is the functionality of the function *htmlentities*?
htmlentities convert all applicable characters to HTML entities, this function is identical to *htmlspecialchars*() in all ways, except with *htmlentities*(), all characters which have HTML character entity equivalents are translated into these entities.

How to increase the execution time of a php script?
Default time allowed for the PHP scripts to execute is 30s defined in the php.ini file. The function used is set_time_limit(int seconds). If the value passed is 0, it takes unlimited time. Modifying the execution time will affect all the sites hosted by the server.

Are PHP objects passed by value or by reference?
Everything is passed by value.

What are the functions for IMAP?

IMAP(Internet Message Access Protocol) is used for communicate with mail servers. It has a number of functions. Few of them are listed below:

```
Imap_alerts  Returns all the imap errors occurred
Imap_body  Reads the message body
Imap_check  Reads the current mail box
Imap_clearflag_full  Clears all flags
Imap_close  close and IMAP stream
Imap_delete  Delete message from current mailbox
Imap_delete_mailbox  Deletes a mailbox
Imap_fetchbody  Fetches body of message
Imap_fetchheader  Fetches header of message
Imap_headers  Returns headers for ALL messages
Imap_mail : send a mail
Imap_sort- Sorts imap messages
```

How can we register the variables into a session?

Use the session_register ($ur_session_var) function.

What is __sleep and __wakeup?

```
__sleep returns the array of all the variables than need to
be saved, while __wakeup retrieves them.
```

Explain how to submit form without a submit button.

```
A form data can be posted or submitted without the button in the following ways:
1. On OnClick event of a label in the form, a JavaScript function
 can be called to submit the form e.g. document.form_name.submit()

2. Using a Hyperlink: On clicking the link, JavaScript function
can be called e.g <a.href= javascript:document.MyForm.submit();">
```

How can we get the properties of an image using php image functions?

```
To know the Image type use exif_imagetype () function
To know the Image size use getimagesize () function
To know the image width use imagesx () function
To know the image height use imagesy() function
```

Write are the statements used to connect PHP with MySQL?

The statements that can be used to connect PHP with MySQL is as follows,

```
<?
$conn = mysql_connect('localhost');
echo $conn;
?>
This statement gets the resource of the localhost.
There are other different ways with which you can
connect to the database and they are as follows:
<?
mysql_connect('db.domain.com:33306','root','user');
mysql_connect('localhost:/tmp/mysql.sock');
mysql_connect('localhost','rasmus','foobar',
true,MYSQL_CLIENT_SSL|MYSQL_CLIENT_COMPRESS);
?>
```

How can we destroy the session, how can we unset the variable of a session, how to get current session id?

session_destroy, session_unset, and session_id() used for destroy session, unset variable of session, get the session id for the current session respectively.

Why PHP is also called as Scripting language?

PHP is basically a general purpose language, which is used to create scripts. Scripts are normal software files that consist of instructions written in PHP language. It tells the computer to execute the file and print the output on the screen. PHP is used for webpages and to create websites, thus included as scripting language.

What are the differences between GET and POST methods in form submitting?

GET and POST are methods used to send data to the server: With the GET method, the browser appends the data onto the URL. With the Post method, the data is sent as "standard input."

After submitting a form, which has the GET method it displays pair of name and value used in the form at the address bar of the url browser but Post method doesn't display these values. For short or small data sending, not containing ASCII characters, then you can use GET Method. But for long data sending, say more then 100 character you can use POST method.

POST method data is sent by standard input (nothing shown in URL when posting while in GET method data is sent through query string. POST is assumed more secure and we can send lot more data than that of GET method is limited (they say Internet Explorer can take care of maximum 2083 character as a query string).

In the GET method the data made available to the action page (where data is received) by the URL so data can be seen in the address bar. Not advisable if you are sending login info like username, password etc. In the post method the data will be available as data blocks and not as query string in case of get method.

On the server side, the main difference between GET and POST is where the submitted is stored. The _GET array stores data submitted by the GET method. The _POST array stores data submitted by the POST method.

Where PHP basically used?

PHP is rapidly gaining the popularity and many companies are switching their current language for this language. PHP is a server side scripting language. PHP executes the instructions on the server itself. Server is a computer where the web site is located. PHP is used to create dynamic pages and provides faster execution of the instructions.

How can we know the count/number of elements of an array?

a) sizeof($urarray) : This function is an alias of count()

b) count($urarray) : interestingly if u just pass a simple var instead of a an array it will return 1.

What is the difference between PHP and JavaScript?

PHP is server side scripting language, which means that it cant interact directly with the user. Whereas, JavaScript is client side scripting language, that is used to interact directly with the user.

What are the different functions in sorting an array?

Sorting functions in PHP are, asort(), arsort() ksort(), krsort(), uksort(), sort(), natsort(), rsort()

How many ways we can pass the variable through the navigation between the pages?
a. Put the variable into session in the first page, and get it back from session in the next page. b. Put the variable into cookie in the first page, and get it back from the cookie in the next page. c. Put the variable into a hidden form field, and get it back from the form in the next page.

What is the maximum length of a table name, database name, and fieldname in mysql?
Database name=64, Table name=64 and Field name=64

What does ODBC(Open DataBase Connectivity) do in context with PHP?
PHP supports many databases like dBase, Microsft SQL Server, Oracle, etc. But, it also supports databases like filePro, FrontBase and InterBase with ODBC connectivity. ODBC is a standard that allows user to communicate with other databases like Access and IBM DB2.

What is meant by MIME(Multi-purpose Internet Mail Extensions)?
WWW ability to recognise and handle files of different types is largely dependent on the use of the MIME standard. The standard provides for a system of registration of file types with information about the applications needed to process them. This information is incorporated into Web server and browser software, and enables the automatic recognition and display of registered file types.

How the web server interprets PHP and interacts with the client?
After installing and configuring the PHP, the Web server looks for PHP code that is embedded in HTML file with its extension. The extensions which are used are .php or .phtml. When web server receives a request for the file with an appropriate extension, HTML statements are processed and PHP statements are executed on the server itself. When the processing gets over the output is being shown in HTML statements.

How PHP statement is different from PHP script?

PHP statements are set of instructions that tell PHP to perform an action. PHP script consists of a series of PHP statements that uses for execution. PHP executes statements one at a time till it reaches the end of the script.

```
PHP statement: echo Hi;
PHP script: if ($a = $b)
{
}
```

What is type casting in PHP? Explain with an example?

PHP automatically store the data and interprets its type according to itself. Type casting is a way to assign the variable according to your need and requirement and not allowing PHP to assign it automatically. To specify the type, it can be used like,

```
$newint = (int) $var1;
$newfloat = (float) $var1;
$newstring = (string) $var1;
```

The value in the variable on the right side of the equal sign is stored in the variable on the left side as the specified type.

What are the different components used in PHP for formatting?

1. %: it tells the start of the formatting instruction.
2. Padding character (pad): is used to fill out the string when the value to be formatted is smaller than the width assigned. Pad can be a space, a 0, or any character preceded by a single quote.
3. –: A symbol meaning to left-justify the characters. If this is not included, the characters are right-justified.
4. width: The number of characters to use for the value. If the value doesn't fill the width, the padding character is used to pad the value. For example, if the width is 5, the padding character is 0, and the value is 1, the output is 00001.
5. dec: The number of decimal places to use for a number. This value is preceded by a decimal point.
6. type: The type of value. Use s(string) for string, f (float) for numbers that you want to format with decimal places.

What is the use of super-global arrays in PHP?

Super global arrays are the built in arrays that can be used anywhere. They are also called as auto-global as they can be used inside a function as well. The arrays with the long names such as $HTTP_SERVER_VARS, must be made global before they can be used in an array, to do this, set in php.ini for long arrays.

What is the difference between $argv and $argc?

These are used to pass the information into the script from outside, help can be taken from the PHP CLI (Command line interface) method. $argv is a variable, always contains at least one element the script name(optionally-other parameter values). $argc is a variable that stores the numbers of elements in $argv. $argc is equal to at least 1, which is saved for the name of the script.

What are the most common caching policy approaches in PHP?

a)Time triggered caching (expiry time stamp after certain time).
b)Content change triggered caching (when content updated).
c)Manually triggered caching.

What is the difference between accessing a class method via -> and via :: ?

:: is scope resolution operator, which does access methods that can perform static operations, i.e. those, which do not require object initialization. In other words, -> is for accessing properties and methods of instantiated objects. The :: is to access static methods, constants or overridden methods.

What is language construct?

Language constructs are builtin constructs in PHP and they can be used like a function. But the basic difference between them is the language constructs can't return the anything. Language constructs can be used with or without parentheses.
Example:
echo(), print(), isset(), unset(), empty(), include(), require(),array(),list()

What is Magic methods ?

Magic methods begin with a double underscore, and this requires changing any user-defined methods or functions that use this naming convention.

List all operations of Array.

a). array_combine() - Creates an array by using one array for keys and another for its values

b). array_diff_uassoc() - Computes the difference of arrays with additional index check which is performed by a user supplied callback function

c). array_udiff() - Computes the difference of arrays by using a callback function for data comparison

d). array_udiff_assoc() - Computes the difference of arrays with additional index check. The data is compared by using a callback function

e). array_udiff_uassoc() - Computes the difference of arrays with additional index check. The data is compared by using a callback function. The index check is done by a callback function also

f). array_walk_recursive() - Apply a user function recursively to every member of an array

g). array_uintersect_assoc() - Computes the intersection of arrays with additional index check. The data is compared by using a callback function

h). array_uintersect_uassoc() - Computes the intersection of arrays with additional index check. Both the data and the indexes are compared by using a callback functions

i). array_uintersect() - Computes the intersection of arrays. The data is compared by using a callback function

What is the difference between public, private, protected, static, transient, final and volatile
Public: Public declared items can be accessed everywhere. Protected: Protected limits access to inherit and parent classes. Private: Private limits visibility only to the class that defines the item. Static: A static variable exists only in a local function scope, but it does not loose its value when program execution leaves the scope. Transient: A transient variable is a variable that may not be serialized. Volatile: A variable that might be concurrently modified by multiple threads should be declared volatile. Variables declared as volatile will not be optimized by the compiler because there value can change at any time.

Chapter 18

Aptitude Questions

In this section, programmatic aptitude questions are given followed by output.

18.1   C++ APTITUDE

```
#include <iostream>
using namespace std;
class Test
    {
    public:
     void method()
{
cout<<"Base"<<endl;
}
};
 class d:public Test
{
public:
void method()
{
cout<< "Derived"<<endl;
}
};
void fun(Test *bObj)
{
bObj->method();
}
int  main()
{
Test bObject;
fun(&bObject);
d dObject;
fun(&dObject);
return 0;
}
```

Output:
Base
Base
Explanation: The method() expects a pointer to a parent class but passed object is a
pointer to a derived class, so it treats the argument only as a base class pointer, hence
corresponding base function is called.

```
#include<iostream>
using namespace std;
#define TOTAL 5
int stk[TOTAL];
int top=0;
class TestStack{
public:
void method(int ele,int op)
{
op==1? ( top==TOTAL?(cout<<"Stack OVERFLOW"<<endl,0):(stk[top++]=ele))
:(op==2)?( top==0?(cout<<"Stack UNDERFLOW"<<endl,0):
(cout<<"Removed Element is="<<stk[--top]<<endl,0)):0;
}
};
int main()
{
TestStack s;
int op,ele;
do{
cout<<"Stack operations"<<endl;
cout<<"Option 1: Push"<<endl;
cout<<"Option 2: Pop"<<endl;
cout<<"Option 3: Exit"<<endl;
cout<<"Please enter operation type"<<endl;
cin>>op;
if(op==1)
{
    cout<<"Please enter an element to Push into TestStack"<<endl;
    cin>>ele;
}
s.method(ele,op);
}while(op<3);
cout<<"Stack elements are"<<endl;
for(int i=0;i<top;i++)
cout<<stk[i]<<endl;
return 0;
}
```

Output:
Stack operations Option 1: Push Option 2: Pop Option 3: Exit Please enter operation
type 1 Please enter an element to Push into TestStack 101 Stack operations Option 1: Push
Option 2: Pop Option 3: Exit Please enter operation type 2 Removed Element is=101
Explanation: Above program does stack(LIFO) operation.

```
#include<iostream>
using namespace std;
class Test
{
public:
        int *p;
        Test(int i)
        {
        p = new int(i);
        }
        ~Test()
        {
        delete p;
        }
        void Method()
        {
        cout << "Value is " << *p;
        }
};
void Func(Test a)
{
cout << "Hello"<<endl;
}
int main()
{
Test t= 100;
Func(t);
t.Method();
return 0;
}
```

Output:
Hello Value is 0
Explanation: The object is passed by value to Func(), control returns from this function, then destructor of the object is called. So when Method() is called it access p which is freed. You can correct this problem by passing the Test object by reference.

```
#include<iostream>
using namespace std;
class Test
        {
        public:
            virtual void TestFun(){ cout<<"Test"; }
};
 class TestDer:public Test
        {
        public:
            void TestFun(){
cout<< "derived class";   }
};
void Method(Test *TestObj)
{
  TestObj->TestFun();
}
int main()
{
Test TestObject;
Method(&TestObject);
TestDer deriObject;
Method(&deriObject);
return 0;
}
```

Output:
Testderived class
Explanation: TestFun is a virtual function which supports run-time polymorphism, hence the function corresponding to the object of derived class is called.

```cpp
#include<iostream>
using namespace std;
class Test
{
public:
int a;
Test(){ a=9;}
};

class TestDer:public Test
{
public:
int b;
TestDer()
{
b=1;
}
};
void Method(Test *arr,int size)
{
for(int i=0; i<size; i++,arr++)
cout<<arr->a;
cout<<endl;
}

int main()
{
Test TestArr[8];
Method(TestArr,8);
TestDer DeriArr[8];
Method(DeriArr,8);
return 0;
}
```

Output:
99999999 91919191

```cpp
#include<iostream>
using namespace std;
class Test
{
    public:
        Test()
{
cout<<"Test()"<<endl;
}
};
int main()
{
Test();
Test t;
Test* t1= new Test;
return 0;
}
```

Output:
Test() Test() Test()
Explanation: In all the above cases, constructor is called by default.

```cpp
#include<iostream>
using namespace std;
class Test
{
    public:
        Test()
                {
                        cout<<"Test()"<<endl;
                }
};
int main()
{
Test Test();
Test;
return 0;
}
```

Output:
No output is displayed.
Explanation: No constructor is invoked.

18.2   JAVA APTITUDE

Output:

```
class T
{
  int i=20;
  T(){
  this(i++);
  }
  T(int i){
  this.i=i;
  }
  public static void main()
  {
      new T();
  }
}
```

Output:
Main.java:5: error: cannot reference i before supertype constructor has been called
this(i++);
Explanation: Cannot refer to an instance field *i* while explicitly invoking a constructor.

```
class T
{
  int i;
  public static void main(String argv[])
  {
      int j= new T().i;
  System.out.println(j+","+new T().i);
  }
}
```

Output:
0,0
Explanation:
Usually all member variables are initialized during creation of the object.

```
class T
{
  public static void main(String argv[])
  {
  int i[]={11,12};
  int j[]=(int[])i.clone();
  System.out.println((i==j)+"aaaaaa");
  i[1]++;
  System.out.println(j[1]);
  }
}
```

Output:
falseaaaaaa
12
Explanation:
The *clone()* function creates a new object with a copy of the original object.

```
import java.util.StringTokenizer;
class TEST
{
  public static void main(String argv[])
  {
  String str="1 2 1.2 3.4 5 6";
  StringTokenizer tokens= new StringTokenizer(str);
  while(tokens.hasMoreElements())
  System.out.println(tokens.nextToken());
  }
}
```

Output:

1
2
1.2
3.4
5
6

Explanation: The StringTokenizer(String str),it constructs a string tokenizer for the specified string. The tokenizer uses the default delimiter set, which is "$\backslash t \backslash n \backslash r \backslash f$": the space character, the tab character, the newline character, the carriage-return character, and the form-feed character. Delimiter characters themselves will not be treated as tokens.

```
class TEST
{
  public static void main(String argv[])
  {
  String str;
  str="123456";
  int j=Integer.valueOf(str).intValue();
  System.out.println(j);
  str="123.456";
  double d=Double.valueOf(str).doubleValue();
  System.out.println(d);
  }
}
```

Output:
123456
123.456
Explanation: The Integer.valueOf (String str), returns an *Integer* object holding the value of the specified String. The argument is interpreted as representing a signed decimal integer, exactly as if the argument were given to the parseInt(java.lang.String) method. The result is an *Integer* object that represents the integer value specified by the string. Double.valueOf(String str) returns a *Double* object holding the double value represented by the argument string *str*.

```
class TEST
{
  public static void main(String[] args)
  {
  int j=fun();
  }
  public int fun(){
  return 1;
  }
}
```

Output:
Compiler Error:cannot make a static reference to the non static method fun() from the TEST.
Explanation: Always static methods(main()) belongs to class,but non static methods belongs to the object of the class.

Solution:
```
class TEST
{
  public static void main(String[] args)
  {
  TEST t=new TEST();
  int i=t.fun();
  }
  public int fun(){
  return 1;
  }
}
```

```
class TEST {
public static void main(String[] args) {
String str1 = new String("ABCD");
String str2 = new String("ABCD");
if (str1 == str2)
System.out.println("SAME");
else
System.out.println("DIFFERENT");
}
}
```

output: DIFFERENT
Explanation: == tests whether the 2 objects are same but not tests whether the value of 2 objects are same.

```
class TEST {
public static void main(String[] args) {
String str1 = "ABCD";
String str2 = "ABCD";
if (str1 == str2)
System.out.println("SAME");
else
System.out.println("DIFFERENT");
}
}
```

output: SAME
Explanation: The 2 strings are literals but not Strings. Here 2 literals are referring to the same object ,hence the output.

```
class TEST {
public static void main(String[] args) {
String str1 = "ABC";
String str2 = "ABCD";
if (str1 == str2)
System.out.println("SAME");
else
System.out.println("DIFFERENT");
}
}
```

output: DIFFERENT
Explanation: Here 2 literals are referring to the different object, hence the output.

```
class TEST {
public static int i;
static{
i=1;
System.out.println("STATIC");
}
public static void main(String[] args) {
new TEST();
System.out.println("main()");
}
TEST()
{
System.out.println("i="+i);
}
}
```

```
output:
STATIC
i=1
main()
```

Explanation: STATIC will be printed first, because static blocks are executed before the main().

```
class TEST {
public static int i;
{
  i=1;
System.out.println("BLOCK");
}
public static void main(String[] args) {
new TEST();
System.out.println("main()");
}
  TEST()
{
System.out.println("i="+i);
}
}
```

```
output:

BLOCK
i=1
main()
```

Explanation: Before the main() block is executed.

```
public class TEST {
static  int f()
{
System.out.println("f()");
return 1;
}
public static void main(String[] args) {
TEST c=new TEST();
TEST.f();
c.f();
}
}
```

```
output: f()
f()
```
Explanation: You can access static members through objects or class name itself.

```
public class TEST {
public static void main(String[] args) {
System.out.println("hi".replace('i', 'h'));
}
}
```

output: hh
Explanation: Replaces i character by h.

```
public class TEST {
TEST  TEST()
{
System.out.println("hi");
TEST t=null;
return t;
}
public static void main(String[] args) {
TEST t= new TEST();
}
}
```

output: Does not print anything
Explanation: Constructors dont have return value hence TEST TEST()... is considered as normal methods instead of a constructor. This methoad has to call explicitly to invoke, however default constructor is executed during object creation.

```
public  class Test{
private static int i=0;
 Test(){
this.i=1000;
 }
 public static void main(String[] args) {
     i=1;
 Test t= new Test();
 System.out.println(i);
 System.out.println(t.i);
 int i=2;
 Test t1= new Test();
 System.out.println(i);
 System.out.println(t1.i);
  }
}
```

Output:

1000
1000
2
1000

Explanation:Local variable will have priority .

```
public class Test{
 public static void main(String[] args) {
     int arr[]=new int[3];
 arr[1]+=arr[1]+=-arr[1]-(-10);
 System.out.println(arr[1]);
   }
}
```

Output:10
Explanation:Expression is evaluated as follows, -arr[1]-(-10)=¿-0+10=¿10 (Arrays values are intitalized with 0 during memory allocation.Minus *Minus=Plus). arr[1]+=arr[1]+=10=¿arr[1]=arr[1]+10=¿arr[1]=0+10=¿arr[1]=10.

```
public class Test{
 public static void main(String[] args) {
     int A = 0x00FF;
   int B = 0x3333;
   System.out.println(A & B & A &B);
   }
}
```

Output:

51
Explanation:
0x00FF; 0000 0000 1111 1111
0x3333; 0011 0011 0011 0011
0x00FF; 0000 0000 1111 1111
0x3333; 0011 0011 0011 0011
=====================
After AND operation:0000 0000 0011 0011
Enabled bits   sum:32+ 16+ 2+1= 51

```
public class Test{
public static void main(String Str[])
{
int i=(2147483647 + 1);
System.out.println(i);
}
}
```

Ouput: -2147483648
Explanation: int can occupy 32 bits in memory (from -2147483648 to +2147483647). In the above program,the sum of (2147483647 + 1)=2147483648, which is higher than +2147483647, this value wrap around and reaches to -ve value.

```
public class Test{
public static void main(String Str[])
{
int i=('A');
System.out.println((char)i);
int j=('A'+'B')-'A';
System.out.println((char)j);
}
}
```

Output: A
B

```
public class Test{
public static void main(String Str[])
{
int i=('A'+'B');
String s=Integer.toString('A'+'B');
System.out.println(i);
System.out.println(s);
}
}
```

output: 131
131 Explanation: ASCII value of 'A' is 65 + ASCII value of 'B' is 66=131

```
public class Test{
private static  boolean b=true;
public static void main(String Str[])
{
System.out.println(Str[0]+"Hello");
if(b){
b=false;
main(new String[]{"Hi"});
}
}
}
```
Output of first run :

```
 <JAVA path>\bin>java Test
Exception in thread "main" java.lang.ArrayIndexOutOfBoundsException: 0
        at Test.main(Test.java:5)
```
Explanation:Array is empty,and program is trying to access the
elements in empty array, hence leading to exception.

Output of Second run :
```
 <JAVA path>\bin>java Test ABC
ABCHello
HiHello
```

Explanation:Using main method for recursion.

```
public class Test{
private static void main(String main[])
{
System.out.println("Hello");
}
}
```
output:Program compiles without error but fails in running by showing a error, "Main method not public".
Explanation: Main method should have public visibility.

```
public class Test{
public static String main[]={"hi"};
public static void main(String main[])
{
System.out.println("main="+main[0]);
}
}
```
Output of first run :

```
<JAVA path>\bin>java Test
Exception in thread "main" java.lang.ArrayIndexOutOfBoundsException: 0
        at Test.main(Test.java:5)
```
Explanation:Array is empty,and program is trying to access the elements in empty array, hence leading to exception.
Output of Second run :
```
<JAVA path>\bin>java Test hello
main=hello
```

Explanation: Array values of main[] is over written by compiler during running of a program.

```
public static void main(String args[])
{
float[] arr = {(float)3.3, (float)4.4,(float)5.5,(float)6.6};
float sum = 0;
for (float f: arr) {
    sum += f;
}
System.out.println("sum="+sum);
}
}
```
output: sum=19.8
Explanation: This program is using enhanced for loop or for-each.The for-each loop is used to access each successive value in a collection of values.

```
public class Test{
public static void main(String args[])
{
int i = 24;
int o = 030;
int h = 0x18;
System.out.println("i="+i);
System.out.println("o="+o);
System.out.println("h="+h);
}
}
output: i=24
o=24
h=24
Explanation: Decimal , octal and hexadecimal values are converted into int value.
```

```
public class Test{
public static void main(String args[])
{
String str1="";
String str2=null;
String str3=str2+str1;
String str4=str1+str2;
String str5=str1+"hi";
String str6="hi"+str2;
if(str1.equals(str2)){
System.out.println("str1=str2");
}
if("".equals(str3)){
System.out.println("str1=str3");
}
System.out.println("str1="+str1);
System.out.println("str2="+str2);
System.out.println("str3="+str3);
System.out.println("str4="+str4);
System.out.println("str5="+str5);
System.out.println("str6="+str6);
}
}
output:

 str1=
str2=null
str3=null
str4=null
str5=hi
str6=hinull
```

Explanation: null is not a empty String.

```
public class Test{
}
```
output:Compiles without error but fails in running.   Exception in thread "main"
java.lang.NoSuchMethodError: main

```
public class Test{
public static void main(String args[])
{
String a=null;
if (a!=null && a.length()>1)
System.out.println("With &&");
if (a!=null & a.length()>1)
System.out.println("With &");
}
}
```
output: Compiles without error but fails in running. Error: Exception in thread "main"
java.lang.NullPointerException at Test.main(Test.java:7)

```
public  class Test{
public  static void main(String[] args) {
    int i = 1;
    int j = 2;
    if (i = j)
        System.out.println("Not equal");
   else
        System.out.println("Equal");
  }
}
```
output:

```
    Exception in thread "main" java.lang.Error: Unresolved compilation problem:
Type mismatch: cannot convert from int to boolean
at Test.main(Test.java:5)
```

Explanation: = is assignment operator, hence if (i = j) causes compilation to fall.

```
class TEST
{
public static void main(String arg[])
{
System.out.println(7*-+("Hello World first ".substring(6)+
"program !").substring(6).length());
}
}
output: -105
```

Explanation: Let us take the display statement,
System.out.println(("Hello World first ".substring(6)+
"program !").substring(6));

=>"Hello World first ".substring(6)? World first
=> (World first program !). Substring(6)?first program !
The length of the string first program ! is 15.
Now come to expression after placing 15 from the length
 of the string, 7*-+15?7*(-15)?-105.

Note:7*-+15 will be translated into 7*(-15) because (minus)*(plus)=minus.

```
import java.util.StringTokenizer;
class TEST
{
public static void main(String arg[])
{
String str="15815.5825835.5";
float sum=0;
StringTokenizer tokens = new StringTokenizer(str);
while(tokens.hasMoreElements()){
sum=sum + Float.valueOf((tokens.nextToken("8")))
.floatValue();
}
System.out.println(sum);
}
}
```

output:91.0
Explanation: StringTokenizer basically used for breaking the string into tokens or words by using delimiters(in this example 8 is the delimiter separator characters). If you don't specify the delimiters, blanks are the default.
A StringTokenizer constructor takes a string to break into tokens and returns a StringTokenizer object for that string. Each time its nextToken() method is called, it returns the next token in that string. This program does the below steps,
a).Extract the tokens from the string by using delimiter.
b).Converting string token into wrapper class Float.
c).Converting Object numbers into primitive numbers(float).
d).Adding all these float values(sum=15+15.5+25+35.5=91.0).
Note: tokens. hasMoreTokens() and tokens.hasMoreElements() performs same operation i.e.,returns TRUE if there are more tokens available from this tokenizer's string,otherwise returns FALSE. Similarly, tokens.nextToken() and tokens.nextElement() performs same operation i.e, returns the next token from the tokenizer's string.

```
class TEST
{
public static int val;
static
{
val=11;
System.out.println("static_val="+val++);
}
public static void main(String arg[])
{
System.out.println("main()_val="+val);
}
}
```

output: static_val=11
main()_val=12
Explanation: Before execution main() function it will execute the static block. Note: A static variable belong to the class, shared by all class instances called class variables.

```
class TEST
{
public static void main(String arg[])
{
int a = 1;
int b = 1;
String aStr= new String("AB");
String bStr= new String("CD");
System.out.println("a+b " + a+++b++);
System.out.println(a+b + " a+b " );
System.out.println("value: " + a + 0 );
aStr+=bStr;
System.out.println("String: " + aStr + ++a + ++b );
}
}
```

output:

```
a+b 11
4 a+b
value: 20
String: ABCD33
```

Explanation: a+++b++ is same as (a++)+(b++).If you write a+b befor (double quotes),then it adds the individual vales and displays the sum.But if you write a+b after (double quotes),then it dispays the individual vales. Note: The + operator is used for both addition and concatenation operation.

```
class TEST
{
public static void main(String arg[])
{
int ch = 6;
switch(ch)
{
case 1: System.out.println( "AB");
case 6: System.out.println(" CD");
default: System.out.println(" GH");
break;
case 4: System.out.println(" EF");
}
}
}
```

output: CD
GH Explanation: Statements will be keep executing until it reaches break statement or until it gets no more statements. Note: Default statement is executed if no case statements match and it can be written in anywhere within switch statement.

```
class TEST
{
public static void main(String arg[])
{
char ch1='h';
char ch2[]={ch1,'i'};
char ch3[]=ch2;
String str1="hi";
String str2[]={"hello"};
String str3[]={new String(new char[]{ch1})};
String str4=new String("hi");
System.out.println(ch1);
System.out.println(ch2);
System.out.println(ch3);
System.out.println(str1);
System.out.println(str2);
System.out.println(str3[0]);
System.out.println(str4);
}
}

output:

h
hi
hi
hi
[Ljava.lang.String;@16930e2
h
hi
```

Explanation: 5th println is printing the string consisting of the name of the class of which the object is an instance along with the unsigned hexadecimal representation of the hash code of the object. Solution:To print the proper string use the index. System.out.println(str2[0]);
Note:String is a predefined class, not an array of characters.
e.g:
String s = "Hello"; // String
char[] a = 'H','e','l','l','o'; // array of characters

```
class TEST
{
public static void main(String arg[])
{
String str = "Hello";
char[] arr = {'H','e','l','l','o'};
String newstr=str.replace('l', 'h');
char[] newarr=arr;
arr[0]='h';
System.out.println(str);
System.out.println(newstr);
System.out.println(arr);
System.out.println(newarr);
}
}
```

output:

```
 Hello
Hehho
hello
hello
```

Explanation: Even though if you apply modification on String object, it will not Modify the original string, instead of it returns a new modified string.
Note: Strings are read-only or immutable, i.e., once an object of the String class is created, the string it contains cannot be changed.

```
    class TEST
{
public static void main(String arg[])
{
System.out.println(5+6);
System.out.println("5"+6);
System.out.println(5+"6");
System.out.println('5'+6);
System.out.println(5+'6');
System.out.println("1"+2+3);
System.out.println(1+2+"3");
}
}
output:

11
56
56
59
59
123
33
Explanation:
11-> 5+6=11
56->6 is appending with string 5.
56->string 6 is appending with 5.
59->ASCII value of 5 is 53,53+6=59
59->ASCII value of 6 is 54,54+5=59
123->same like above.
33->same like above.
```

```
    class TEST
{
public static void main(String arg[])
{
int i=10;
String str1 = "x = " + i;
String str2 = 2.7 + "";
String str3 = 2.7;
String str4 = "" + 2.7;
String str5 = "" + i/2.7;
System.out.println(str1+str2+str4+str5);
}
}
```
output: Compiler error at line no.8. java.lang.Error: Unresolved compilation problem:
Type mismatch: cannot convert from double to String Cause and Solution: String str3 =
2.7; is illegal as str3 is a string.The java.text.DecimalFormat class provides many ways to
format numbers into strings, including number of fraction digits and etc.
Output: After removing the line no.8,you will get the below output.   x =
102.72.73.7037037037037033
Note:To round up the floating point numbers ,can be used DecimalFormat or the
Math.round method.

```
    class TEST
{
public static void main(String arg[])
{
int a = 10, b = 30;
System.out.println(a + b);
System.out.println(a + b + "1");
System.out.println("2" + a + b);
System.out.println("3" + a * b);
System.out.println("3" + a - b);
System.out.println("4" + a / b);
}
}
```

output:Compiler error at line no.10. java.lang.Error: Unresolved compilation problem: The operator - is undefined for the argument type(s) String, int Cause :Based on the operators priority,3+a is becoming an string .Therefore doing String integer is not allowed.

```
Solution: System.out.println("3" +(a - b));
Output:After correcting the above line, you will get the below result.
40
401
21030
3300
3-20
40
```

Note: In the expression ,if there is a + operator , so the expression is evaluated left-to-right unless there were another operator with higher precedence, the sub-expression involving that operator would be evaluated first and rest is next.

```
    class TEST
{
public static void main(String arg[])
{
short s1=32767,s2=-32768;
int i=(byte)++s1;
int j=(byte)--s2;
int k=s1/(byte)s2;
int l=s2/(byte)s1;
System.out.println("i="+ i+" j="+j);
System.out.println("k="+ k+" l="+l);
}
}
```

output: Run time error at line no.9. java.lang.ArithmeticException: / by zero at TEST.main(TEST.java:9) Cause: Divide by zero error. Solution:For run time exception handing you can use try-catch . After correcting the above line, you will get the below output.

```
    class TEST
{
public static void main(String arg[])
{
short s1=32767,s2=-32768;
int i=(byte)++s1;
int j=(byte)--s2;
int k=s1/(byte)s2;
int l=s2/s1;
try{
l=s2/(byte)s1;
}catch(ArithmeticException ex)
{
System.out.println("ERROR:DIVIDE BY ZERO");
}
System.out.println("i="+ i+" j="+j);
System.out.println("k="+ k+" l="+l);
}
}
```

output: ERROR:DIVIDE BY ZERO i=0 j=-1 k=32768 l=0
Note:Mainly ArithmeticException caused by math errors. The exception handling mechanism has fallowing tasks,

```
->Hit the exception.
->Throw the exception.
->Catch the exception.
->Handle the exception.
```

```
    class TEST
{
public static void main(String arg[])
{
String str1 = 2.7 + "";
String str2 = "" + 2.7;
String str3 = "2.7";
String str4 = "3.7";
if(str1==str2)
System.out.println("1");
if(str1.equals(str2))
System.out.println("2");
if(str1==str3)
System.out.println("3");
if(str1.equals(str3))
System.out.println("4");
if(str1==str4)
System.out.println("5");
if(str1.equals(str4))
System.out.println("6");
}
}

output:

1
2
3
4
```

```
    class TEST
{
public static void main(String arg[])
{
byte b1=127,b2=-128;
b1++;b2--;
System.out.println("b1="+ b1+" b2="+b2);
}
}

output: b1=-128 b2=127
```

```
    class TEST
{
public static void main(String arg[])
{
int b1=127,b2=-128;
int i=(byte)++b1;
int j=(byte)--b2;
int k=b1;
int l=b2;
System.out.println("i="+ i+" j="+j);
System.out.println("k="+ k+" l="+l);
}
}
```

output:

```
 i=-128 j=127
k=128 l=-129
```

```
class TESTAA {
int i;
private int j;
void set(int a, int b) {
i = a;
j = b;
}
}
class TESTBB extends TestAA{
int k=20;
}
class TEST{
public static void main(String args[]){
TestBB b=new TestBB ();
b.set(10,20);
System.out.println("The value of i"+b.i+"j="+b.j +"k="+b.k);
}
}
```
output: Exception in thread "main" java.lang.Error: Unresolved compilation problem:
The field TestAA.j is not visible at Test.main(Test.java:16)
Explanation: In class TESTAA int j is defined as private, even tough TestBB is a subclass
of TestAA it cannot inherit private members of super class TESTAA, class member that
has been declared as private will remain private to its class hence it is not accessible by
any code outside its class, including subclasses.

```
public class TEST {
 String str = "Test";
 Test(){}
 Test(String st){
 str=st;
 }
 void method() {
 InnerClass i = new InnerClass();
  i.innermethod();
  Test t=new Test("Hi");
  System.out.println(t.str);
  i.innermethod();
 }
 class InnerClass {
    public void innermethod() {
    System.out.println(str);
      }
     }

 public static void main(String[] av) {
  Test p = new Test();
  p.method();
  }

}

output:

Test
Hi
Test
```

Explanation: Objects that are instances of an inner class exist within an instance of the outer class. An inner class is associated with an instance of its surrounding class and has direct access to that object's methods and fields.

```
public class TEST {
 public static void main(String args[])
 {
 int a=1,b=2,c;
 System.out.println("Sum="+a+b+c);
 }
}
```
output: Exception in thread "main" java.lang.Error: Unresolved compilation problem: The local variable c may not have been initialized at Test.main(Test.java:5)
Explanation: Variable c has to initialize to some value.

```
public class TEST {
 int x=10;
 Test(){
 this(2);
 }
 Test(int x){
 this(x,x);
 }
 Test(int x,int y){
 this();
 this.x=x+y;
 }

 public static void main(String args[])
 {
  Test t=new Test();
  System.out.println("value ="+t.x);
  main(args);
 }
}
```

output:

```
 Exception in thread "main" java.lang.Error: Unresolved compilation problems:
Recursive constructor invocation Test(int)
Recursive constructor invocation Test(int, int)
Recursive constructor invocation Test()
at Test.init(Test.java:4)
at Test.main(Test.java:16)
```

Explanation: Recursive constructors are not allowed but methods are allowed.

```
public class TEST {
 int x=10;
 Test(){
 this(x);
 }
 Test(int a){
x=a;
 }
 public static void main(String args[])
 {
  Test t=new Test();
  System.out.println("value ="+t.x);
 }
}
```

output:

```
 Exception in thread "main" java.lang.Error: Unresolved compilation problem:
Cannot refer to an instance field x while explicitly invoking a constructor
at Test.<init>(Test.java:4)
at Test.main(Test.java:11)
```

Explanation: It is not possible to refer to not existing field before its declaration. Normally constructors will execute before any code, hence x is not allowed in constructor. public

```
    class TEST {
static int i = 10; int j=0;
public  void Test (int k) {
System.out.println(i);
}
public static void main (String args []) {
Test t=new Test(i);
t.Test(i);
}
}
```
output:

```
Exception in thread "main" java.lang.Error: Unresolved compilation problem:
The constructor Test(int) is undefined
at Test.main(Test.java:7)
```

Explanation: public void Test (int k) is not a constructor as it is having return type , it is a normal method hence Test(int) is not defined in this class.
public

```
   class TEST {
public void divOperation(int x, int y) {
try {
x=x / y;
}catch (Exception e) {
System.out.print("Caught exception, ");
} finally {
System.out.println("hit finally!");
}
}
public static void main (String args []) {
Test t=new Test();
t.divOperation(1,0);
t.divOperation(0,1);
}
}
```

output: Caught exception, hit finally! hit finally!
Explanation: The finally block always executes when the try block exit irrespective of exception throws.

```
class Vehicle {
public void speed() {
System.out.println("Vehicle-speed");
}
}
class Car extends Vehicle {
public void speed() {
System.out.println("Car-speed");
}
}

public class TEST {
public static void main (String args []) {
Vehicle v=new Vehicle();;
Vehicle v1=new Vehicle();;
Car c= new Car();
v.speed();
c.speed();
v = c;
v.speed();
c=(Car)v1;
c.speed();
}
}
```
output: Vehicle-speed
Car-speed
Car-speed
Exception in thread "main" java.lang.ClassCastException: Vehicle cannot be cast to Car at Test.main(Test.java:20)
Explanation: c=(Car)v1; is not allowed .

```
interface transport {
public void speed() ;
}
class Vehicle implements transport{
public void speed() {
System.out.println("Vehicle-speed");
}
}
class Car extends Vehicle    {
public void speed() {
System.out.println("Car-speed");
}
}
public class TEST {
public static void main (String args []) {
Vehicle v=new Vehicle();
    transport v1=new Vehicle();
    transport c1=new Car();
Car c= new Car();
v.speed();
c.speed();
v = c;
v.speed();
c1=v1;
c1.speed();
}
}
output:

    Vehicle-speed
Car-speed
Car-speed
Vehicle-speed
```

```
class Employee{
String name;
int sal;
Employee(String name , int sal){
this.name=name;
this.sal=sal;
}
public void method(){
System.out.println(this.name);
System.out.println(this.sal);
}
}
public  class TEST {
public static void main (String args []) {
Employee emp=null;
try{
emp = new Employee("ABC", 1200);
emp.method();
}finally{
System.gc();
emp.method();
}
 }
 }
output:

ABC
1200
ABC
1200
```

```
public class TEST {
public void method1(int x) {
loop: for (int i = 1; i < 3; i++){
for (int j = 1; j < 3; j++) {
System.out.println("Method1:"+i * j);
if (x == 1) {
break loop;
}
}
}
}
public void method2(int x) {
for (int i = 1; i < 3; i++){
for (int j = 1; j < 3; j++) {
System.out.println("Method2:"+i * j);
if (x== 1) {
break ;
}
}
}
}
public static void main (String args []) {
Test t=new Test();
t.method1(1);
t.method2(1);
 }
 }
```

output:

```
 Method1:1
Method2:1
Method2:2
```

Explanation: The unlabeled break statement terminates the innermost for loop, switch, while loop, or do-while loop statement, but a labeled break terminates an outer statement.

```
public  class TEST {
public void method1(int x) {
switch (x) {
default:
System.out.print(1+",");
case 1:
System.out.print(2+",");
case 2:
case 3:
System.out.print(3+",");
case 4:
System.out.print(4);
}
}
public void method2(int x) {
switch (x) {
case 1:
System.out.print(2+",");
case 2:
case 3:
System.out.print(3+",");
case 4:
System.out.print(4+",");
default:
System.out.print(1);
}
}


public static void main (String args []) {
Test t=new Test();
t.method1(5);
System.out.println("");
t.method1(1);
System.out.println("");
t.method2(5);
System.out.println("");
t.method2(1);
  }
  }
```

output:

```
 1,2,3,4
2,3,4
1
2,3,4,1
```

Explanation: The default section handles all values that aren't explicitly handled by the switch case s. In the above program break statement is missing hence control flow is not terminated the switch.

```
class A {
public A (String str) {
System.out.println(str);
}
}
public class TEST extends A {
public static void main(String args []) {
Test t=new Test();
}
}
```
output: Exception in thread "main" java.lang.Error: Unresolved compilation problem:
Implicit super constructor A() is undefined for default constructor. Must define an
explicit constructor at Test.init(Test.java:6) at Test.main(Test.java:8)
Explanation: Default constructor A() is missing in class A.

```
public class  Test {
public static void Test() {
print(true);
}
public static void print(boolean f) {
f = !f;
if (f = true) {
System.out.println("TRUE");
}
else {
System.out.println("FALSE");
}

}
public static void main(String args []) {
Test();
}
}
```
output: TRUE
Explanation: f = !f; =¿ f=false but if statement has f = true (assignment operator not ==
operator), it makes f=true , hence prints TRUE.

```
public class  Test {
public  Test() {
method();
}
public   void method1() {
System.out.println("A");
}
public static void method() {
System.out.println("B");
method1();
}
public static void main(String args []) {
Test t=new Test();
}
}
```
output: Exception in thread "main" java.lang.Error: Unresolved compilation problem:
Cannot make a static reference to the non-static method method1() from the type Test at
Test.method(Test.java:10)at Test.¡init¿(Test.java:3) at Test.main(Test.java:13)
Explanation: In Java, static methods or class methods cannot call non-static methods.
An instance of the class is required to call its methods e.g method1( )and static methods
are not associated with an instance .

```
public class  Test {
public   void method() {
StringBuffer sb = new StringBuffer("ABC");
String s = new String("ABC");
if(sb.equals(s)){
System.out.println("A");
}
if(sb.toString().equals(s)){
System.out.println("B");
}
if(sb.equals(new StringBuffer(s))){
System.out.println("C");
}
if(sb.toString().equals(new StringBuffer(s).toString())){
System.out.println("D");
}
}
public static void main(String args []) {
Test t=new Test();
t.method();
}
}
```
output: B
D
Explanation: sb.equals(s)=¿sb and s are different objects, hence comparison is invalid.
sb.toString().equals(s)=¿The value of sb is converted into String and comparing with
String s, this makes exact comparison. sb.equals(new StringBuffer(s))=¿Comparing
Same object types but different object references, here it is not comparing String
values. sb.toString().equals(new StringBuffer(s).toString())=¿converted into String and
comparing both values, this makes exact comparison.

```
public class  Test {
Test(){
System.out.println("default constructor");
}
Test(int i){
System.out.println("constructor,i="+i);
}
static {
System.out.println("static block");
Test();
}

public static void Test() {
System.out.println("static method");
}
public static void main(String args []) {
Test t = new Test();
t.Test();
Test t1 = new Test(10);
t1.Test();
}
}
```

output:

```
 static block
static method
default constructor
static method
constructor,i=10
static method
```

Explanation: Static block will be executed once when the class is first loaded into the Java virtual machine.

```
public class  Test {
public static void main(String args []) {
   System.out.println("A");
 /*System.out.println("B");
   System.out.println("C");
 /*System.out.println("D");*/
   System.out.println("E");
}
}
output: A
E
```

```
import java.util.Vector;
public class  Test {
public static void main(String args []) {
String str1 = "A";
String str2 = "B";
Vector vct = new Vector();
vct.add(str1);
vct.add(str2);
String str3 = vct.elementAt(0) + vct.elementAt(1);
System.out.println(str3);
}
}
```
output: Exception in thread "main" java.lang.Error: Unresolved compilation problem:
The operator + is undefined for the argument type(s) java.lang.Object, java.lang.Object
at Test.main(Test.java:9)
Explanation: Type casting is required during object assignment, e.g., vct.elementAt(0) +
vct.elementAt(1); should be written as (String)vct.elementAt(0) + vct.elementAt(1);

```
public class  Test {
public static void main(String args []) {
String str = new String("ABC");
String s[]= {new String("AB"),new String("CD")};
int i=str.length();
int j=s.length;
System.out.println("i="+i);
System.out.println("j="+j);
}
}
```

output: i=3
j=2
Explanation: The length keyword is used to find out the array length and length() method
is used find out the String length.

```
class A{
 public  abstract void method(){
 System.out.println("Hi");
 }
 }
public class  Test extends A {
public static void main(String args []) {
Test t=new Test();
t.method();
}
}
```

output: Exception in thread "main" java.lang.Error: Unresolved compilation problems: The type A must be an abstract class to define abstract methods The abstract method method in type A can only be defined by an abstract class Abstract methods do not specify a body.

Explanation: If any method in the class is declared as abstract then the class has to be declared abstract and the method has to be implemented in the following subclass(s). Hence declare above class as abstract clas.

```
abstract class A{
 abstract void method();
 }
public class  Test extends A {
void method1(){
System.out.println("Hi");
}
public static void main(String args []) {
Test t=new Test();
t.method();
}
}
```

output: Exception in thread "main" java.lang.Error: Unresolved compilation problem: The type Test must implement the inherited abstract method A.method()

Explanation: Abstract methods of base class have to be implemented in the derived subclass(s).Hence method() has to implement in class TEST.

```
abstract class A{
  void method(){
  System.out.println("Class A");
  }
 }
public class  Test extends A {
void method(){
System.out.println("Hi");
}
public static void main(String args []) {
Test t=new Test();
t.method();
A t1=new A();
}
}
```

output: Exception in thread "main" java.lang.Error: Unresolved compilation problem: Cannot instantiate the type A at Test.main(Test.java:13)
Explanation: When a class is declared as abstract we can't instantiate it. Remove A t1=new A(); to avoid compiler error.

```
abstract class A{
  void method(){
  System.out.println("Class A");
  }
 }
public class  Test extends A {
void method(){
System.out.println("Hi");
}
public static void main(String args []) {
Test t=new Test();
t.method();
((A)t).method();
}
}
```
output: Hi
Hi
Explanation: Object t is instance of Test, which is derived from base class A, method() is implemented in subclass and hence it will be will be executed.

```
abstract class A{
  void method(){
  System.out.println("Class A");
  }
 }
public class  Test extends A {
public static void main(String args []) {
Test t=new Test();
t.method();
((A)t).method();
}
}
```
output: Class A
Class A
Explanation: Default behavior is considered when there is no implementation in derived/subclasses. interface interf public void method();

```
abstract class A implements interf{
  public void method(){
  System.out.println("Class A");
  }
 }
public class  Test extends A {
private void method(){
System.out.println("Hi");
}
public static void main(String args []) {
Test t=new Test();
t.method();
}
}
```
output: Exception in thread "main" java.lang.Error: Unresolved compilation problem: Cannot reduce the visibility of the inherited method from A
Explanation: If abstract class has public method and its visibility cannot be reduced in the inherited method of a class, here private void method() should be converted into public.

```
interface  interf{
 public abstract void method();
}
abstract class A {
  public abstract void method();
 }

public class  Test extends A implements interf{
public void method(){
System.out.println("Hi");
}
public static void main(String args []) {
Test t=new Test();
((interf)t).method();
((((t)))).method();
}
}
```

output: Hi
Hi

```
interface  interf{
 public abstract int method();
}
abstract class A {
 public abstract void method();
 }

public class  Test extends A implements interf{
public void method(){
System.out.println("Hi");
}
public int method(){
System.out.println("Hello");
return 0;
}
public static void main(String args []) {
Test t=new Test();
((interf)t).method();
t.method();
}
}
```
output: Exception in thread "main" java.lang.Error: Unresolved compilation problem:
at Test.main(Test.java:16)

```
interface  interf{
 public abstract void method(){
 System.out.println("Hi");
 }
}
public class  Test implements interf{
public void method(){
System.out.println("Hello");
}
public static void main(String args []) {
Test t=new Test();
t.method();
((interf)t).method();
}
}
output:
Hello
Hello
```

Explanation: Even though interface method has a body, it does not prevent to compile and run the program.

```
interface  interf{
 public abstract void method(){
 System.out.println("Hi");
 }
}
public class  Test implements interf{
public static void main(String args []) {
Test t=new Test();
((interf)t).method();
}
}
```

output: Exception in thread "main" java.lang.Error: Unresolved compilation problem: The type Test must implement the inherited abstract method interf.method()

Explanation: Interface will never provide default behavior (abstract class will provide default behavior), hence all methods in the interface class are abstract by default and it has to be implemented in implementer classes.

```
public class  Test {
static{
try{

}catch(Exception exe){
try{

}catch(Exception e){

}finally{
}
}
finally{
System.out.println("Hi");
}
}
public static void main(String args []) {
}
}
output: Hi
Explanation: Static block will be executed first by default without explicit calling and
finally block is executed irrespective of control flow in the try-catch block.
```

```
public class  Test {
static private final int k=10;
static final  private  int l=10;
final static private  int m=10;
final  private static int n=10;
private static  final int o=10;
private final static   int p=10;

public  void  method( final int k){
System.out.println(k);//local value gets high priority
System.out.println(l);
System.out.println(m);
System.out.println(n);
System.out.println(o);
System.out.println(p);
}
public static void main(String args []) {
Test t = new Test();
t.method(20);
}
}
```

output:

```
 20
10
10
10
10
10
```

Explanation: Basically private, static and final are modifiers keywords and they can be placed in any order.

```
class A{
public void methodA(){
System.out.println("A");
}
}

public class  Test extends A {
public  void  methodA( ){
System.out.println("Test");
super.methodA();
}

public  void  methodA(int i ){
System.out.println("i="+i);
}
public  void  methodA( char c){
System.out.println("c="+c);
}

public static void main(String args []) {
Test t = new Test();
t.methodA();
t.methodA(10);
t.methodA('A');
((A)t).methodA();
A a = new A();
a.methodA();
}
}

output:

 Test
A
i=10
c=A
Test
A
A
```

Explanation: class TEST is overriding a method called methodA( ) and has overloading methods like, methodA(int i) and methodA(char i). Base class or super calss method can be called by using super keyword.

```
class A{
public final void methodA(){
System.out.println("A");
}
}
public class  Test extends A {
public  final void  methodA( ){
System.out.println("Test");
super.methodA();
}
public static void main(String args []) {
Test t = new Test();
t.methodA();
}
}
```
output: java.lang.VerifyError: class TEST overrides final method methodA()
Explanation: Final method cant be overridden.

```
final class A{
public   void methodA(){
System.out.println("A");
}
}
public class  Test extends A {
public  final void  methodA( final int  i ){
System.out.println("i="+i++);
}
public static void main(String args []) {
Test t = new Test();
t.methodA(10);
}
}
```

output: Exception in thread "main" java.lang.Error: Unresolved compilation problem:
at Test.main(Test.java:10)
Explanation: Final variable acts like a constant and value cant be changed from its
initiated value, similarly final class cant get subclassed.

```
final abstract class A{
public   abstract void methodA();
}
public class  Test extends A {
public   final void  methodA(  int  i ){
System.out.println("i="+i++);
}
public static void main(String args []) {
Test t = new Test();
t.methodA(10);
}
}
```

output: Exception in thread "main" java.lang.Error: Unresolved compilation problem:
at Test.main(Test.java:8)
Explanation: A class can be either final or abstract; you cannot use both keywords
together.

```
class A{
 void A(){
 System.out.println("A");
}
   A(){
   System.out.println("B");
    }
}
public class  Test extends A {

Test(){
super();
super.A();
}
public static void main(String args []) {
Test t = new Test();
t.A();
}
}
```

output: B
A
A
Explanation: super(); calls constructor of base class, super.A(); calls the method of base
class.

```
class A{
private static int i=10;
public  static int j=20;
}
public class  Test  {
public static void main(String args []) {
System.out.println(A.i);
System.out.println(A.j);
}
}
```
output: Exception in thread "main" java.lang.Error: Unresolved compilation problem: The field A.i is not visible at Test.main(Test.java:7)

Explanation: Public variable/method is accessible to members of any class. Private variable/method cannot access from outside the class. abstract class A private void method1() System.out.println("A"); public abstract void method2() ;

```
public class  Test extends A {
public void method2(){
System.out.println("B");
}
public static void main(String args []) {
Test t=new Test();
t.method1();
t.method2();
}
}
```
output: Exception in thread "main" java.lang.Error: Unresolved compilation problem: The method method1() from the type A is not visible at Test.main(Test.java:13)

Explanation: Visibility modifier in abstract class can be public or protected.

```
interface  inter {
public    void method() ;
}
public class  Test implements inter  {
public static void main(String args []) {
Test t=new Test();
t.method();
}
}
```
output: Exception in thread "main" java.lang.Error: Unresolved compilation problem: The type Test must implement the inherited abstract method inter.method()at Test.method(Test.java:4) at Test.main(Test.java:7)

Explanation: A class, which implements an interface, must implement all of the methods of interface.

```
interface  inter {
public  final  void method() ;
}
public class  Test implements inter  {
public void method(){
System.out.println("A");
}
public static void main(String args []) {
Test t=new Test();
t.method();
}
}
output:   Exception  in  thread  "main"  java.lang.Error:   Unresolved  compilation
problem:  Cannot override the final method from inter at Test.method(Test.java:5) at
Test.main(Test.java:10)
Explanation: Final methods cannot be overridden, implicitly JAVA override interface
methods.
```

```
interface  inter {
private  void method() ;
}
public class  Test implements inter  {
public void method(){
System.out.println("A");
}
public static void main(String args []) {
Test t=new Test();
t.method();
}
}
output: A
Explanation: Though methods of interface should have public or abstract visibility but
JAVA still compile and runs the above program.
```

```
interface  inter {
public  void method() ;
}
class  A implements inter{
}
public class  Test extends A  {
public void method(){
System.out.println("A");
}
public static void main(String args []) {
Test t=new Test();
t.method();
}
}

output: A
```

```
interface  inter {
public   void method() ;
final private int i=10;
}
public class  Test implements inter {
public final void method(){
System.out.println("A");
}
public static void main(String args []) {
Test t=new Test();
t.method();
}
}
output: java.lang.ClassFormatError: Illegal field modifiers in class inter:0x1B
Explanation: Only public, static and final are permitted for variables/fields in interface.
```

```
class A {
A(){
System.out.println("A");
}
}
public class  Test extends A {
public Test(){
System.out.println("B");
}
public static void main(String args []) {
Test t=new Test();
}
}
output: A
```
B Explanation: No need to make a call to default constructor of base class, because it will be supplied automatically.

```
public Test(){
super();
System.out.println("B");
}
is same as
public Test(){
System.out.println("B");
}
```

```
class A {
A(){
System.out.println("A");
}
}
public class  Test extends A {
public Test(){
System.out.println("B");
super();
}
public static void main(String args []) {
Test t=new Test();
}
}
```
output: Exception in thread "main" java.lang.Error: Unresolved compilation problem: Constructor call must be the first statement in a constructor at Test.¡init¿(Test.java:9) at Test.main(Test.java:12)
Explanation: Calling the constructor for the base class must be the first statement in the body of a constructor.

```
class A {
A(){
System.out.println("A");
}
A(char c ){
System.out.println(c);
}
}
public class  Test extends A {
public Test(){
super();
}
public Test(char i){
super(i);
}
public  Test(int i,int j){
this();
}
public  Test(int i,int j,int k){
this('c');
}
public static void main(String args []) {
Test t=new Test();
}
}

output: A
```

```
class A {
A(){
System.out.println("A");
}
}
public class  Test extends A {
public  Test(){
super();
super();
}
public static void main(String args []) {
Test t=new Test();
}
}
output:  Exception in thread "main" java.lang.Error:  Unresolved compilation prob-
lem:Constructor call must be the first statement in a constructor at Test.¡init¿(Test.java:9)
at Test.main(Test.java:12)
```

```
public class  Test extends Object {
public static void main(String args []) {
Test t=new Test();
Object o=new Object();
if(t.getClass().equals(o.getClass())){
System.out.println("Hi");
}else{
System.out.println("Hello");
}
}
}

output: Hello
Explanation: All classes in JAVA directly or indirectly inherit from Object class.
```

```
import java.util.*;
public class TEST{
  public static void main(String[] args) {
    TreeMap <Integer, String>mp = new TreeMap<Integer, String>();
    TreeMap mp1 = new TreeMap();
    mp.put(5, "Z");
    mp.put(7, "A");
    mp.put(2, "B");
    mp1.put("Z", "12");
    mp1.put("A", "2");
    mp1.put("D", "32");
    mp1.put("E", "22");
    System.out.println("Keys of mp: " + mp.keySet());
    System.out.println("Values of mp: " + mp.values());
    System.out.println("Keys of mp1: " + mp1.keySet());
    System.out.println("Values of mp1: " + mp1.values());
  }
}
output:

 Keys of mp: [2, 5, 7]
Values of mp: [B, Z, A]
Keys of mp1: [A, D, E, Z]
Values of mp1: [2, 32, 22, 12]
```

Explanation: Content of tree map will be sorted by either their natural order, or by a Comparator using keys.

```java
import java.util.*;
public class TEST{
  public static void main(String[] args) {
    TreeMap mp = new TreeMap();
    mp.put(3, "Z");
    mp.put(1, 3);
    mp.put(2, 'c');
    System.out.println("Keys of mp: " + mp.keySet());
    System.out.println("Values of mp: " + mp.values());
  }
}
output:

Keys of mp: [1, 2, 3]
Values of mp: [3, c, Z]
```

```java
import java.util.*;
public class TEST{
  public static void main(String[] args) {
    TreeMap mp = new TreeMap();
    mp.put(3, "Z");
    mp.put('c', 3);
    mp.put("A", 'c');
    System.out.println("Keys of mp: " + mp.keySet());
    System.out.println("Values of mp: " + mp.values());
  }
}
output:        Exception    in    thread    "main"    java.lang.ClassCastException:       at
Test.main(Test.java:6)
Explanation: Data type for keys should be same across the given tree map.
```

```java
import java.util.*;
public class TEST{
  public static void main(String[] args) {
    TreeMap mp = new TreeMap();
    mp.put(String.valueOf(3), "Z");
    mp.put(Integer.valueOf('c').toString(), 3);
    mp.put("A", 'c');
    System.out.println("Keys of mp: " + mp.keySet());
    System.out.println("Values of mp: " + mp.values());
  }
}
output:

 Keys of mp: [3, 99, A]
Values of mp: [Z, 3, c]
```

```
import java.text.DecimalFormat;
import java.text.NumberFormat;
import java.util.*;
public class TEST{
  public static void main(String[] args) {
    TreeMap mp = new TreeMap();
    int c=10;
    NumberFormat format = new DecimalFormat("1000");
    mp.put(format.format(Integer.parseInt( "11")),  String.format("%06d", 12));
    mp.put(format.format(Integer.parseInt( "21")), 'B');
    mp.put(format.format(Integer.parseInt( "13")), c);
    System.out.println("Keys of mp: " + mp.keySet());
    System.out.println("Values of mp: " + mp.values());
  }
}
output:

 Keys of mp: [1011, 1013, 1021]
Values of mp: [000012, 10, B]
```

Explanation: Numeric and String formatting is used.

```
import java.util.*;
public class TEST{
public static void main(String[] args) {
TreeMap mp = new TreeMap();
mp.put("GH", new Float(123.45));
mp.put("AC", new Float(456.78));
mp.put("FD", new Float(789.12));
Set set = mp.entrySet();
Iterator i = set.iterator();
while(i.hasNext()) {
Map.Entry me = (Map.Entry)i.next();
System.out.print(me.getKey() + ": ");
System.out.println(me.getValue());
mp.remove("AC");
}
}
}
```
output: AC: 456.78   Exception   in   thread   "main"
java.util.ConcurrentModificationException at Test.main(Test.java:11)
Explanation: Interpreter has detected concurrent modification of an object where as such
modification is not permissible.

```
import java.util.*;
class TEST {
public static void main(String args[]) {
HashMap mp = new HashMap();
mp.put("A", new Integer(123));
mp.put("A", new Integer(123));
mp.put("Z", new Integer(456));
mp.put("Z", new Integer(456));
mp.put("B", new Integer(789));
mp.put("B", new Integer(789));
System.out.println("Keys of mp: " + mp.keySet());
System.out.println("Values of mp: " + mp.values());
}
}
output:

 Keys of mp: [A, B, Z]
Values of mp: [123, 789, 456]
```

Explanation: Duplicates are eliminated.

```
import java.util.*;
 class TEST {
public static void main(String args[]) {
HashMap mp = new HashMap();
mp.put("A", new Integer(123));
mp.put("", new Integer(124));
mp.put(null, new Integer(125));
Set set = mp.entrySet();
Iterator i = set.iterator();
while(i.hasNext()) {
Map.Entry me = (Map.Entry)i.next();
System.out.print(me.getKey() + ": ");
System.out.println(me.getValue());
}
}
}
output:

 null: 125
: 124
A: 123
```

```
    class TEST {
public  String method(int i){
return (""+i);
}
public static void main(String args[]) {
System.out.println(method(100));
}
}
```
output: Exception in thread "main" java.lang.Error: Unresolved compilation problem:
Cannot make a static reference to the non-static method method(int) from the type Test
at Test.main(Test.java:6)
Explanation: A static method can only call other static method.

```
import java.util.*;
class TEST {
public static void main(String args[]) {
HashMap mp = new HashMap();
mp.put("A", new Integer(1));
mp.put("", new Integer(2));
mp.put(null, new Integer(3));
mp.put("",null);
mp.put(null, "");
mp.put(null, null);
System.out.println(mp.get("") );
System.out.print(mp.get(null) );
}
}
```
output: null
null
Explanation: Maps can accept a null key and null values and latest values overlaps
previous value if duplicate existed .

```
import java.util.*;
class TEST extends HashMap {
public static void main(String args[]) {
HashMap mp = new HashMap();
mp.put(' ', new Integer(1));
System.out.println(mp.get('\b') );
}
}
```
output: null

```
import java.util.*;
class TEST {
public static void main(String args[]) {
Hashtable ht = new Hashtable();
Enumeration en;
String str;
ht.put("4", new Double(12.12));
ht.put("3", new Double(34.56));
ht.put("6", new Double(78.89));
en = ht.keys();
while(en.hasMoreElements()) {
str = (String) en.nextElement();
ht.remove(str);
System.out.println(str + ": " +
ht.get(str));
}
}
}
output:

 6: null
4: null
3: null
```

Explanation: In Hash Table, you can change the iteration and no exception will be thrown. Like the Hash Map classes, Hashtable does not directly support iterators. Hence, the program uses an enumeration to display the contents of ht. However, you can obtain set-views of the hash table, which permits the use of iterators.

```
import java.util.*;
class TEST {
public static void main(String args[]) {
Hashtable <String, Double>ht = new Hashtable<String, Double>();
Enumeration <String>en;
String str;
ht.put("4", new Float(12.12));
ht.put("3", new Double(34.56));
ht.put("6", new Double(78.89));
en = ht.keys();
while(en.hasMoreElements()) {
str = (String) en.nextElement();
System.out.println(str + ": " +
ht.get(str));
}
}
}
output: Exception in thread "main" java.lang.Error: Unresolved compilation problem:
The method put(String, Double) in the type

Hashtable<String,Double>
```

```
import java.util.*;
class TEST {
public static void main(String args[]) {
Hashtable <String, Double>ht = new Hashtable<String, Double>();
ht.put("4", new Double(12.12));
ht.put("3", new Double(34.56));
ht.put("6", new Double(78.89));
Hashtable <String, Double>ht1 = new Hashtable<String, Double>(2);
ht1.put("7", new Double(12.12));
ht1.put("9", new Double(34.56));
ht1.put("8", new Double(78.89));
Hashtable <String, Double>ht2 = new Hashtable<String, Double>(2,(float).1);
ht2.put("2", new Double(12.12));
ht2.put("1", new Double(34.56));
ht2.put("3", new Double(78.89));
HashMap mp = new HashMap();
mp.put("A", new Integer(1));
mp.put("B", new Integer(2));
mp.put("C", new Integer(3));
Hashtable <String, Double>ht3 = new Hashtable<String, Double>(mp);

System.out.println("Keys of mp: " + ht.keySet());
System.out.println("Values of mp: " + ht.values());
System.out.println("Keys of mp: " + ht1.keySet());
System.out.println("Values of mp: " + ht1.values());
System.out.println("Keys of mp: " + ht2.keySet());
System.out.println("Values of mp: " + ht2.values());
System.out.println("Keys of mp: " + ht3.keySet());
System.out.println("Values of mp: " + ht3.values());
}
}
output:

Keys of mp: [6, 4, 3]
Values of mp: [78.89, 12.12, 34.56]
Keys of mp: [9, 8, 7]
Values of mp: [34.56, 78.89, 12.12]
Keys of mp: [3, 2, 1]
Values of mp: [78.89, 12.12, 34.56]
Keys of mp: [A, C, B]
Values of mp: [1, 3, 2]
```

```
import java.util.*;
class TEST {
public static void main(String args[]) {
Hashtable <String, Double>ht = new Hashtable<String, Double>(2,(float)0.0);
ht.put("7", new Double(12.12));
ht.put("9", new Double(34.56));
ht.put("8", new Double(78.89));
System.out.println("Keys of mp: " + ht.keySet());
System.out.println("Values of mp: " + ht.values());
}
}
```
output: Exception in thread "main" java.lang.IllegalArgumentException: Illegal Load: 0.0 at java.util.Hashtable.¡init¿(Unknown Source) at Test.main(Test.java:4) Explanation: Creating a hash table that has an initial size specified by size and a fill ratio specified by fillRatio.

```
import java.util.EnumMap;
enum enm{ONE,TWO ,THREE}
public class TEST {
 void test() {
        emp.put(enm.THREE, 1000);
        emp.put(enm.ONE, 2000);
        System.out.println(emp.get(enm.ONE)*emp.get(enm.THREE));
    }
    private EnumMap<enm,Integer> emp = new EnumMap<enm,Integer>(enm.class);
    public static void main(String[] args) {
        Test eg = new Test();
        eg.test();
    }
}
```
output: 2000000

```
import java.util.*;
class TEST {
public static void main(String args[]) {
HashSet <String>hs = new HashSet<String>();
HashSet <String>hs1 = new HashSet<String>();
hs.add("4");
hs.add("1");
hs.add("3");
hs.add("2");
hs1=hs;
System.out.println(hs.equals(hs.remove("10")));
System.out.println("hs:"+hs);
System.out.println(hs1.equals(hs));
System.out.println("hs1:"+hs1);
hs.remove("1");
System.out.println("hs:"+hs);
System.out.println("hs1:"+hs1);
}
}
output:

false
hs:[3, 2, 1, 4]
true
hs1:[3, 2, 1, 4]
hs:[3, 2, 4]
hs1:[3, 2, 4]
```

Explanation: A HashSet is an unsorted, unordered Set, it uses the hashcode of the object being inserted.

```
import java.util.*;
class TEST {
public static void main(String args[]) {
HashSet hs = new HashSet();
hs.add("4");
hs.add(hs);
hs.add("2");
hs.add("2");
System.out.println("hs:"+hs);
}
}
output: hs:[2, (this Collection), 4]
```
Explanation: Duplicates are eliminated in HashSet.

```
import java.util.HashSet;
import java.util.Iterator;
public   class TEST
   {
   public static void main( String[] args )
     {
        HashSet hs = new HashSet();
        hs.add("1");
        hs.add("2");
        hs.add("3");
        Iterator iter = hs.iterator();
        while(iter.hasNext())
        {
           System.out.println(iter.next());
           iter.remove();
        }
     }
   }
output: 3
2
1
```

```
import java.util.HashSet;
import java.util.Iterator;
public   class TEST
   {
   public static void main( String[] args )
     {
        HashSet <String>hs = new HashSet<String>();
        hs.add("1");
        hs.add("2");
        hs.add("3");
        Iterator <String>iter = hs.iterator();
        {
           System.out.println(iter.next());
           iter.remove();
        }
     }
   }
output: 3
```

```
import java.util.Iterator;
import java.util.TreeSet;
public class TEST
   {
  public static void main( String[] args )
    {
      TreeSet<String>hs = new TreeSet<String>();
       hs.add("1");
       hs.add("2");
       hs.add("3");
       Iterator <String>iter = hs.iterator();
       while(iter.hasNext())
       {
          System.out.println(iter.next());
          iter.remove();
       }
    }
   }
output: 1
2
3
```

```
import java.util.Iterator;
import java.util.TreeSet;
public class TEST
   {
  public static void main( String[] args )
    {
    TreeSet<TreeSet>hs = new TreeSet<TreeSet>();
       hs.add(hs);
       Iterator iter = hs.iterator();
       while(iter.hasNext())
       {
          System.out.println(iter.next());
          iter.remove();
       }
    }
   }
output: [(this Collection)]
```

```java
import java.util.Iterator;
import java.util.TreeSet;
public class TEST
   {
   public static void main( String[] args )
     {
        TreeSet <TreeSet<TreeSet<TreeSet>>>hs = new TreeSet();
        TreeSet hs1 = new TreeSet();
        hs1.add("Hi");
         hs.add(hs1);
         Iterator iter = hs.iterator();
         while(iter.hasNext())
         {
            System.out.println(iter.next());
            iter.remove();
         }
     }
   }
output: [Hi]
```

```java
import java.util.Iterator;
import java.util.LinkedHashMap;
import java.util.Set;

public class TEST {
public static void main(String[] args) {
LinkedHashMap hm = new LinkedHashMap();
hm.put("","A");
hm.put("","B");
hm.put("","C");
Set st = hm.keySet();
Iterator itr = st.iterator();
while(itr.hasNext()){
System.out.println(itr.next());
}
}
}
output: No output generated from this program.
```

```
import java.util.*;
class TEST {
   public static void main(String args[]) {
       LinkedHashSet hs = new LinkedHashSet();
       hs.add("3");
       hs.add("2");
       hs.add("1");
       hs.add("5");
       System.out.println(hs.contains('1'));
   }
}

output: false
```

```
import java.util.EnumSet;
public class TEST {
  enum Letter  { A,B,C,D };

  public static void main(String[] args) {
    EnumSet<Letter> i = EnumSet.of(Letter.A, Letter.B);
    EnumSet<Letter> j = EnumSet.range(Letter.C, Letter.D);
    EnumSet<Letter> k = EnumSet.complementOf(j);
    EnumSet<Letter> l = EnumSet.allOf(Letter.class);
    if(i.contains(Letter.A))
      System.out.println("A is there !");
    if(!i.contains(Letter.C))
      System.out.println("C is not there !");
    for(Letter s : j)
     System.out.println(s);
  }

  public static boolean canGoToMoes(EnumSet<Letter> m) {
    return !m.contains( EnumSet.range(Letter.A, Letter.B) );
  }
}
output:

A is there !
C is not there !
C
D
```

```
public class TEST extends Thread implements Runnable{
public static int count=0;
 public Test(String str) {
super(str);
}

public void run()
{
for (int i = 0; i < 10; i++) {
            count=count+i;
}
System.out.println("val="+count);
}

public static void main(String[] args){
new Test("ABC").start();
    new Test("DEF").start();
}
}
output: val=45
val=90
Explanation: Sum of numbers from 0 to 9.
```

```
public class TEST extends Thread{
public static int count=0;
 public Test(String str) {
super(str);
}
public static void run()
{
        System.out.println("val="+count);
}
public static void main(String[] args){
new Test("ABC").start();
}
}
output: This program does not print anything.
```

```
public class TEST extends Thread{
public static int count=0;
 public Test(String str){
super(str);
}
public static void run(){
        System.out.println("val="+count);
}
public static void main(String[] args){
Test t=new Test("ABC");
t.start();
t.run();
}
}
output: Exception in thread "main" java.lang.Error: Unresolved compilation problem:
This static method cannot hide the instance method from Thread at Test.run(Test.java:6)
at Test.main(Test.java:12)
```

```
interface interf1{
abstract public void method();
}
interface interf2 extends interf1{
abstract public void method();
}
class A implements interf1{
 public void method(){
 System.out.println("1");
 }
}
public class TEST extends A implements interf1, interf2{
public void method(){
System.out.println("2");
}
public static void main(String[] args){
Test t=new Test();
t.method();
A a=new A();
a.method();
((interf1)t).method();
((interf2)t).method();
((interf1)a).method();
((interf2)a).method();
}
}
output:

 2
1
2
2
1
```

Exception in thread "main" java.lang.ClassCastException: A cannot be cast to interf2 at
Test. main (Test.java: 24)

Explanation: Class A is not implementing interf2, hence above exception is thrown.

```
 interface interf1{
abstract public void method();
}
interface interf2 extends interf1{
abstract public void method();
}
class A {
A(int i){
this.method();
}
A(){
A a=new A(1);
a.method();
}
public void method(){
System.out.print("1,");
}
}
public class TEST extends A implements interf1, interf2{
Test(){
super();
}
public void method(){
System.out.print("2,");
}
public static void main(String[] args){
Test t=new Test();
t.method();
A a=new A();
a.method();
((interf1)t).method();
((interf2)t).method();
}
}
output: 1,1,2,1,1,1,2,2,
```

```
public class TEST implements Runnable
{
  private String name;
  private long time;

  public Test(String name, long time)
  {
    this.name = name;
    this.time = time;
  }

  public static void main (String[] args)
  {
    Thread t = new Thread(new Test("ABC",1));
    t.setDaemon(true);
    t.start();
    Thread t1 = new Thread(new Test("DEF",1));
    t1.setDaemon(true);
    t1.start();
    try
    {
        System.in.read();
    }
    catch (Exception e)
    {
        System.out.println("Exception "+e);
    }
  }

  public void run()
  {
  int i=0;
    do
    {
      System.out.println(name);
      try {
        Thread.sleep(time);
        }
      catch (Exception e)
      {
          System.out.println("Exception "+e);
      }
    }while(i--!=0);
  }
}
output:

 1)ABC
DEF
Or
2)ABC
DEF
```

```
import java.io.*;
import java.util.*;
public class TEST
{
 public static void main (String[] args) throws java.io.IOException
  {
   String str;
   int i = 1;
   BufferedReader br = new BufferedReader (new FileReader
    ("D:/test/abcTest/src/Test.java"));
   while(true){
 str= br.readLine();
 if(str==null)
 break;
   System.out.println ("Line$\sharp1$"+i+++":"+str);
   }
   }
}
output:

 Line$\sharp1$:import java.io.*;
Line$\sharp1$2:import java.util.*;
Line$\sharp1$3:public class TEST
Line$\sharp1$4:{
Line$\sharp1$5: public static void main (String[] args) throws
 java.io.IOException
Line$\sharp1$6: {
Line$\sharp1$7:  String str;
Line$\sharp1$8:  int i = 1;
Line$\sharp1$9:  BufferedReader br = new BufferedReader (new FileReader
 ("D:/test/abcTest/src/Test.java"));
Line$\sharp1$10:  while(true){
Line$\sharp1$11:  str= br.readLine();
Line$\sharp1$12:  if(str==null)
Line$\sharp1$13:  break;
Line$\sharp1$14:   System.out.println ("Line$\sharp1$"+i+++":"+str);
Line$\sharp1$15:  }
Line$\sharp1$16:  }
Line$\sharp1$17:}
```

```java
import java.io.*;
public class TEST
{
 public static void main (String[] args) throws java.io.IOException
 {

  String str;
  boolean flag = true;
  BufferedReader br = new BufferedReader (new InputStreamReader (System.in));
  FileWriter fw = new FileWriter ("D:/test/abcTest/src/Text.txt");
  BufferedWriter bw = new BufferedWriter (fw);
  PrintWriter pw = new PrintWriter (bw);
  while ( flag )
     {
       System.out.println ("Enter the input String.");
       str = br.readLine();
       if (str.length() == 0)
        flag = false;
  else
  pw.println (str);
     }
  pw.close();
  System.out.println ("Your Data is here:");
  int i = 1;
  BufferedReader br1 = new BufferedReader (new FileReader
  ("D:/test/abcTest/src/Text.txt"));
  while(true){
 str= br1.readLine();
 if(str==null)
 break;
  System.out.println ("Line$\sharp1$"+i+++":"+str.toUpperCase());
  }
  }
}
output:

 Enter the input String.
aaaaa
Enter the input String.
bbbbb
Enter the input String.
CCCCC
Enter the input String.
<ENTER nothing>
Your Data is here:
Line$\sharp1$1:AAAAA
Line$\sharp1$2:BBBBB
Line$\sharp1$3:CCCCC
```

```
public class TEST {
    public static void main (String[] args) throws Exception {
      System.out.println(0/0);
      throw new Exception("Test Exception");
    }
}
```
output: Exception in thread "main" java.lang.ArithmeticException: / by zero at Test.main(Test.java:3)
Explanation: Control flow has not reached throw Exception code, it is failed before reaching this line.

```
public class TEST {
public static void main(String args[])
{
Runtime rt = Runtime.getRuntime();
int numOfProcessors = rt.availableProcessors();
System.out.println(numOfProcessors + " processor(s) are available to JVM");
}
}
```

output: 2 processor(s) are available to JVM
Explanation: availableProcessors()method of Runtime get the number of processors available to the current JVM.

```
public class TEST {
public static void main(String args[])
{
Runtime rt = Runtime.getRuntime();
System.out.println("Maximum memory available to JVM:"+rt.maxMemory()+"bytes");
}
}
```
output: Maximum memory available to JVM:259522560 bytes
Explanation: maxMemory() method of Runtime calculates the maximum amount of memory available to the current JVM.

```
public class TEST {
public static void main(String args[])
{
Runtime.getRuntime().gc();
System.out.println("Running Garbage Collector...");
}
}
```
output: Running Garbage Collector...
Explanation: gc() method of Runtime class suggest the JVM to run garbage collection.

```
import java.util.Properties;
public class TEST {
public static void main(String[] args) {
String OS = System.getProperty("os.name");
String JavaVersion = System.getProperty("java.specification.version");
Properties properties = System.getProperties();
if(OS != null)
{
if(OS.toLowerCase().indexOf("windows") != -1)
System.out.println("Your OS is Windows...");
else
System.out.print("Your OS is not windows...");
}
System.out.println("Java Version : " + JavaVersion);
System.out.println("Properties of System:");
properties.list(System.out);
}
}
output:

Your OS is Windows...
Java Version : 1.6
Properties of System:
--listing properties --<prints all properties of current system>
```

```
public  class TEST {
public static void main(String[] args) {
StringBuffer strbuf = new StringBuffer(new String(new String("ABC ")));
strbuf.append("DEF");
System.out.println("Append Operation:"+strbuf);
int len = strbuf.length();
System.out.println("Length Operation:"+len);
String str = strbuf.substring(5);
System.out.println("Substring Operation: " + str);
String str1 = strbuf.substring(0,5);
System.out.println("Substring Operation: " + str1);
strbuf.replace(0,5,"AB");
System.out.println("Replace Operation: " + strbuf);
strbuf.insert(3,"ABCD ");
System.out.println("Insert Operation:"+strbuf);
strbuf.deleteCharAt(1);
System.out.println("Delete Operation:"+strbuf);
strbuf.reverse();
System.out.println("Reversed Operation: " + strbuf);
}
}
output:

 Append Operation:ABC DEF
Length Operation:7
Substring Operation: EF
Substring Operation: ABC D
Replace Operation: ABEF
Insert Operation:ABEABCD F
Delete Operation:AEABCD F
Reversed Operation: F DCBAEA
```

```
import java.util.LinkedList;
public class TEST {
public static void main(String[] args) {
LinkedList<String> ll = new LinkedList<String>();
LinkedList<LinkedList<String>> lll = new LinkedList<LinkedList<String>>();
ll.add("B");
ll.add("C");
ll.add("D");
ll.addFirst("A");
ll.addLast("E");
lll.add(ll);
System.out.println(lll.contains("F") && lll.remove().equals("A"));
System.out.println("Linked List:" + lll);
}
}
output: false
Linked List:[[A, B, C, D, E]]
```

```
import java.util.StringTokenizer;
public class TEST {
public static void main(String[] args) {
StringTokenizer st1 = new StringTokenizer("AB|CD", "|");
while(st1.hasMoreTokens()){
System.out.println(st1.nextToken());
}
StringTokenizer st2 = new StringTokenizer("EF|GH");
while(st2.hasMoreTokens()){
System.out.println(st2.nextToken("F"));
}
}
}

output:

 AB
CD
E
|GH
```

```
import java.util.StringTokenizer;
public class TEST {
public static void main(String[] args) {
StringTokenizer st = new StringTokenizer("Hello world !", " ");
String strReversedLine="";
while(st.hasMoreTokens()){
 strReversedLine = (st.nextToken().toLowerCase()
 + " " + strReversedLine.toUpperCase()).replace("HELLO", "Hi");
}
System.out.println(strReversedLine);
}
}
output: ! WORLD HI
```

```
public class TEST {
public static void main(String[] args) {
Double i = Double.valueOf(Float.valueOf(Integer.valueOf(Short.valueOf("1")
.toString()).toString()).toString());
System.out.println(i);
}
}

output: 1.0
```

```
public class TEST {
public static void main(String[] args) {
Double i = Double.valueOf(Float.valueOf(Integer.valueOf(Short.valueOf("1.0")
.toString()).toString()).toString());
System.out.println(i);
}
}
output: Exception in thread "main" java.lang.NumberFormatException: For input string:
"1.0"at java.lang.NumberFormatException.forInputString
```

```
import java.util.ArrayList;
import java.util.Collections;
import java.util.Comparator;

class intComparator implements Comparator{
public int compare(Object obj1, Object obj2){
int obj1Val = ((Integer)obj1).intValue();
int obj2Val = ((Integer)obj2).intValue();
if( obj1Val > obj2Val )
return 1;
else if( obj1Val < obj2Val )
return -1;
else
return 0;
}
}
public class TEST {
public static void main(String[] args) {
ArrayList <Integer>arrList = new ArrayList<Integer>();
arrList.add(2);
arrList.add(4);
arrList.add(1);
arrList.add(3);
Collections.sort(arrList,new intComparator());
System.out.println(arrList);
}
}

output: [1, 2, 3, 4]
```

```
import java.util.ArrayList;
import java.util.Collections;
import java.util.Comparator;
public class TEST {
public static void main(String[] args) {
ArrayList <Integer>arrList = new ArrayList<Integer>();
arrList.add(2);
arrList.add(4);
arrList.add(1);
arrList.add(3);
Comparator <Integer>comparator = Collections.reverseOrder();
Collections.sort(arrList,comparator);
System.out.println(arrList);
}
}

output: [4, 3, 2, 1]
```

```
import java.util.ArrayList;
import java.util.Vector;
public class TEST {
public static void main(String[] args) {
Vector <String>vect = new Vector<String>();
vect.add("A");
vect.add("C");
vect.add("E");
ArrayList <String>arrList = new ArrayList<String>();
arrList.add("B");
arrList.add("D");
vect.addAll(1,arrList);
vect.remove("A");
for(int i=0; i<vect.size(); i++)
System.out.print(vect.get(i)+" ");
}
}
output: B D C E
```

```
import java.util.*;
import java.lang.*;
import java.io.*;
class Program {
private int id;
public Program (int id) {
this.id = id;
}
public int hashCode() {
return id;
}
public boolean equals (Object obj) {
return (this == obj) ? true : super.equals(obj);
}
public boolean equals (int obj) {
return (this.id == obj) ? true : super.equals(obj);
}
}
public class Test {
public static void main(String[] args) {
Program p1 = new Program(100);
Program p2 = new Program(100);
Program p3 = new Program(200);
System.out.print(p1.equals(p1) + " ");
System.out.print(p1.equals(p2) + " ");
System.out.print(p1.equals(100) );
}
}

output: true false true
```

```
import java.util.*;
import java.lang.*;
import java.io.*;

class B {
void method() {
System.out.println("B");
}
}
class A extends B{
void method() {
System.out.println("A");
}
}
public class Test
{
public static void main (String[] args) throws java.lang.Exception
{
A A = new A();
((B)A).method();
A C = new A();
((B)C).method();
B B = new B();
((B)A).method();
B D = new B();
((B)D).method();
}
}
```

output: A A A B

```
import java.util.*;
public class Test {
public static void main(String[] args) {
List<Integer> L = new <Integer>ArrayList();
L.add(11);
L.add(22);
L.add(33);
L.add(44);
L.add(Integer.valueOf(L.get(-0).toString()));
System.out.println(L);
}
}
```

output: [11, 22, 33, 44, 11]

```
import java.util.Scanner;

class Test
{
public static void main (String[] args)
{
Scanner S1 = new Scanner(System.in);
String ch = S1.next();
System.out.println("1st str=" + ch);
int ch1 = S1.nextInt();
System.out.println("2nd int=" + ch1);
float ch2 = S1.nextFloat();
System.out.println("3rd float=" + ch2);
}
}

Input:
10 20 30.33

output: 1st str=10 2nd int=20 3rd float=30.33
```

```
import java.util.*;
import java.lang.*;
import java.io.*;
class Clz {
int a = 10;
String method1() {
return "clz1";
}
protected static String method2 () {
return "clz2";
}
}

class Test extends Clz {
int a = 20;
String method1() {
return "test1";
}

public static String method2() {
return "test2";
}

void method() {
Clz m = new Test();
System.out.print(m.method1()+ " "+ m.method2() +" "+ m.a);
}

public static void main (String[] args) {
new Test().method();
}
}
```

output: test1 clz2 10

```
public class Test{
public static void main(String srgs[]){
static int i=10;
System.out.println(i);
}
}
```

output: Exception in thread "main" java.lang.Error: Unresolved compilation problem:
Illegal modifier for parameter i; only final is permitted
at Test.main(Test.java:3)
Explanation: Static variables are defined at class level but it can't be declared inside a method.

```
public class Test {
public static void main(String[] args) {
int a=1000,b=2000;
a^=b^=a^=b;
System.out.println(a+":"+b);
a=1000;b=2000;
b=a^=b=b^a^b;
System.out.println(a+":"+b);

}
}
output: 0:1000 0:0
```

```
class T
{
    final public int method(int a, int b) { return 0; }
}
class T1 extends T
{
    public int method(int a, int b) {return 1; }
}
public class Test
{
    public static void main(String args[])
    {
        T1 b = new T1();
        System.out.println(b.method(10, 20));
    }
}

output: Exception in thread "main" java.lang.VerifyError: class T1 overrides final
method method.(II)I
Explanation: Cannot override final method.
```

```
public class Test {
public static void main(String[] args) {
int a=10,b='a';
System.out.println(true ?a:b);
System.out.println(false?a:b);
}
}

output: 10 97
```

```
class Test
{
    public static void main(String [] args)
    {
        Test t = new Test();
        t.m();
    }

    void m()
    {
        int [] a1 = {10,20,30};
        int [] a2 = method(a1);
        System.out.println(a1[0] + a1[1] + a1[2]);
        System.out.println(a2[0] + a2[1] + a2[2]);
    }

    int [] method(int [] a)
    {
        a[1] = 40;
        return a;
    }
}
output: 80 80
```

```
class Test
{
    public static void main(String [] args)
    {
        Test t = new Test();
        t.m();
    }

    void m()
    {
        String str1 = "5678";
        String str2 = method(str1);
        System.out.println(str1 + str2);
    }

    String method(String s1)
    {
        s1 = s1 + "1234";
        System.out.println(s1);
        return "1234";
    }
}
output: 56781234 56781234
```

```
public class Test {
public static void main(String[] args) {
int a=123456;
short b=0;
System.out.println(b+=a);
}
}
```

output: -7616

```
class Test
{
    public static void main(String [] args)
    {
        int i = 0x80000000;
        System.out.println(i);
        i = i >>> 31;
        System.out.println(i);
        i = i << 31;
        System.out.println(i);
    }
}
```

output: -2147483648 1 -2147483648

```
public class Test {
public static void main(String[] args) {
System.out.println(0*20000000 +0xabcafebe);
System.out.println(0*20000000L+0xabcafebeL);
}
}
```
output: -1412759874 2882207422

```
class Test
{
    public static void main(String [] args)
    {
        int i = 22;
        float f = (float)22.1;
        boolean b = (i == f);
        System.out.println(b);
        int c=20;
        String str = (c < 15) ? "Hi" : (c < 22)? "hello" : "1234";
        System.out.println(str);
    }
}
```

output: false hello

```
class Test
{
    public static void main(String [] args)
    {
     int i= 10;
        int j= 10;
        for (int a = 0; a < 10; a++)
        {
            if (( ++i > 2 ) && (++j > 2))
            {
                i++;
            }
        }
        System.out.println(i + " " + j);

        int k= 20;
        int l= 20;
        for (int a = 0; a < 10; a++)
        {
            if (( ++k > 2 ) || (++l > 2))
            {
                k++;
            }
        }
        System.out.println(k + " " + l);

        int m = 21 & 22;
        int n = m ^ 2;
        System.out.println( n | 10 );
    }
}
```

output: 30 20 40 20 30

```
class Test
{
    public static void main(String [] args)
    {
    boolean a = true;
    boolean b = false;
    boolean c = true;
    if ( a & b | b & c | b )
        System.out.print("A");
    if ( a & b | b & c | b | a )
        System.out.println("B");
}
}

output:B
```

```
class Test
{
static int stat;
    public static void main(String [] args)
    {
            Test t = new Test();
            t.method();
            System.out.println(stat);
    }
        void method()
        {
            int a = 20;
            m(a);
            System.out.print(a + " ");
        }

        void m(int a)
        {
            a = a*2;
            stat = a;
        }
}

output: 20 40
```

```
class A
{
    byte i;
}

class Test
{
    public static void main(String [] args)
    {
        Test t = new Test();
        t.method();
    }

    void method()
    {
        A a = new A();
        System.out.println(a.i);
        A b = m(a);
        System.out.println(a.i + " " + b.i);
    }

    A m(A a)
    {
        a.i = 10;
        return a;
    }
}

output: 0 10 10
```

```
class Test
{
    boolean [] b = new boolean[10];
      int i = 0;

      void method(boolean [] a, int i)
      {
          a[i] = true;
          ++i;
      }

      public static void main(String [] args)
      {
          Test t = new Test();
          t.method(t.b, 0);
          t.method(t.b, 1);
          t.test();

          int a = 10, b = 1;
          a <<= b;
          System.out.println(a);
      }

      void test()
      {
          if ( b[0] && b[1] | b[2] )
              i++;
          if ( b[1] && b[(++i - 1)] )
              i += 20;
          System.out.println(i);
      }
}

output: 22 20
```

```
public class Test {
public static void main(String[] args) {
for (byte b = Byte.MIN_VALUE; b <= Byte.MAX_VALUE; b++) {
if (b == Byte.MIN_VALUE || b==Byte.MAX_VALUE)
System.out.println(b);
}
}
}

output: Printing infinite values of -128(min) and 127(max).
```

```
public class Test {
public static void main(String[] args) {
try {
} finally {
System.out.println("First:"+Long.toHexString(0x100L + 0xabcdef));
}

try {
System.exit(0);
} finally {
System.out.println("Second:"+Long.toHexString(0x100L + 0xabcdef));
}
}
}
```

output: First:abceef
Explanation: System.exit(0); stops all program threads immediately hence it does not execute finally block.

```
public class Test {
public static void main(String[] args) {
Runtime r = Runtime.getRuntime();
System.out.println("Max memory in MB: " + r.maxMemory() / 1024);
System.out.println("Allocated memory in MB: " + r.totalMemory() / 1024);
System.out.println("Free memory in MB: " + r.freeMemory() / 1024);
System.out.println( r.maxMemory()-r.totalMemory()== r.freeMemory());
}
}
```

output: Max memory in MB: 886592 Allocated memory in MB: 59776 Free memory in MB: 58837 false

```
import java.math.BigDecimal;
public class Test {
public static void main(String[] args) {
int var1=101; float var2=(float) 100.100;
System.out.println(var1-var2);
System.out.println(101-100.100);
System.out.println(new BigDecimal(var1-var2));
System.out.println(new BigDecimal(101-var1));
}
}
output: 0.9000015 0.9000000000000057 0.90000152587890625 0
```

```
public class Test {
public static void main(String[] args) {
final int var1=1000001; final float var2=(float) 10000.100;
long l=(long) (var1*var2);
System.out.println(var1*var2+":"+l);
}
}
output: 1.00001096E10:10000109568
```

```
public class Test {
public static void main(String[] args) {
int var1=101, var2=100;
System.out.println((var1%2==1) + ":"+(var2%2==1));
System.out.println((var1%2!=0) + ":"+((var1&1)!=1)+ ":"+((var2&1)!=1));
}
}

output: true:false true:false:true
```

```
public class Test {
public static void main(String[] args) {
System.out.println((int)(char)(byte)-1);
System.out.println((byte)(char)(int)-1);
System.out.println((float)(int)(byte)-1);
System.out.println((double)(byte)(int)-1);
}
}
output: 65535 -1 -1.0 -1.0
```

```
public class Test {
public static void main(String[] args) {
Object a=123456;
String b="0";
System.out.println(a+=b);
}
}

output: 1234560
```

```
public class Test {
public static void main(String[] args) {
Object a=123456;
String b="0";
System.out.println(a+=b);
    a=a+b;
System.out.println(a+=b);
}
}
output: 1234560 123456000
```

```
public class Test {
public static void main(String[] args) {
int a='a';
int b=1;
System.out.println(a);
System.out.println(a+=b);
System.out.println((char)(a+=b));
    a=a+b;
System.out.println(a+=b);
}
}
output: 97 98 c 101
```

```
public class Test {
public static void main(String[] args) {
int a='a';
int b=1;
System.out.println((char)a+b+":"+a);
}
}
output: 98:97
```

```
public class Test {
public static void main(String[] args) {
int a='A';
int b=1;
System.out.println(a+'\n');
System.out.println(a+'A');
System.out.println(a+"A");
}
}
output: 75 130 65A
```

```
public class Test {
public static void main(String[] args) {
String a="123";
char b[]={'A','B','C'};
Object c=(Object)b;
System.out.println(a+":"+b+":"+c);
}
}
output: 123:[C@7926b165:[C@7926b165
```

```
class Test{
    static {
    System.out.println("static block executed...");
    }
    public static void main(String[] args) {
     System.out.println("main method executed...");
    }
}
output: static block executed... main method executed...
```

```
public class Test
{
    public static void method ()
    {
        System.out.print("A ");
        throw new RuntimeException();
    }
    public static void main(String [] args)
    {
        try
        {
            System.out.print("B ");
            method();
        }
        catch (Exception re )
        {
            System.out.print("C ");
        }
        finally
        {
            System.out.print("D ");
        }
        System.out.println("E ");
    }
}
output: B A C D E
```

```
class Test
{
    public static void main(String [] args)
    {
        Test t = new Test();
        t.m1();
    }
    void m1()
    {
        boolean b1 = false;
        boolean b2 = m(b1);
        System.out.println(b1 + " " + b2);
    }

    boolean m(boolean b1)
    {
        b1 = true;
        return b1;
    }
}
output: False true
```

```
class Test {
public void M(int i, int j)
{
System.out.println("A="+ i+j);
}

public void M(int i, double j)
{
System.out.println("B="+ i+j);
}

public void M(double i, double j)
{
System.out.println("C="+ i+j);
}
public static void main(String str[]){
Test t = new Test();
t.M(1,1);
t.M(1,1.1);
t.M(1.1,1.1);
}
}
output: A=11 B=11.1 C=1.11.1
```

```
class Test{
    static {
    String str[]={"ABC","DEF"};
    main(str);
    System.out.println("static block executed...");
    }
    public static void main(String[] args) {
    System.out.println("main method executed..."+args[0]);
    }
}
```
output: main method executed...ABC static block executed... Exception in thread "main"
java.lang.ArrayIndexOutOfBoundsException: 0 at Test.main(Test.java:8)

```
class Test{
    public static void main(String[] args) {
    System.out.println("a\u0024.length()+\u0024b".length());
    }
}
```
output: 14

```
class Test{
    public static void main(String[] args) {
    char a='\n';
    char b=0X000A;
    System.out.println(a+":"+b);
    }
}
```
output: :

```
import java.util.Random;
class Test{
    public static void main(String[] args) {
    Random r= new Random();
    switch(r.nextInt(3)){
    case 1:
    System.out.println("Hi");
    case 2:
    System.out.println("Hello");
    case 3:
    System.out.println("Bye");
    default:
    System.out.println("Good Night");
    }
  }
}
```
output: Good Night (output is uncertain).

```java
class Test{
    public static void main(String[] args) {
     int a=0;
     int c=100;
     int d=0;
     int e=100;

     for(int b=0;b<100;b++)
     {
     a=a++; c--; d=++d; e=--e;
     }
     System.out.println(a+":"+c+":"+d+":"+e);
  }
}
```
output: 0:0:100:0
Explanation: ++ and - - does assignment of value post increment and decrement operation.

```java
class Test{
    public static void main(String[] args) {
     boolean i=true, j=false;
         if( i )
         {
             System.out.println("1");
         }
         else if(i && j)
         {
             System.out.println( "1 && 2");
         }
         else
         {
             if ( !j )
             {
                 System.out.println( "1") ;
             }
             else
             {
                 System.out.println( "2" ) ;
             }
         }
     }
}
```
output: 1

```
class Test{
    public static void main(String[] args) {
      float j=2;
      switch((int)j)
      {
          default:
              System.out.println("hi");
      }
    }
}
output: Hi
```

```
class Test
{
    public static void main(String [] args)
    {
        Test t = new Test();
        t.m1();
    }

    void m1()
    {
        String str1 = "A";
        String str2 = m(str1);
        System.out.println(str1 + " " + str2);
    }

    String m(String str)
    {
        str = str + "B";
        System.out.print(str + " ");
        return "C";
    }
}
output: AB A C
```

```
class Test{
    public static void main(String[] args) {
      int j=1;
      if(j)
      {
          System.out.println("hi");
      }
      while(j)
      {
          System.out.println("hi");
      }
    }
}
```
output: Cannot compile program. Exception: Exception in thread "main" java.lang.Error: Unresolved compilation problems: Type mismatch: cannot convert from int to boolean Type mismatch: cannot convert from int to Boolean

```
class Test{
public static int a;
    public static int M(int x)
    {
        System.out.print("M ");
        a = x;
        return x;
    }
    public static int N(int z)
    {
        System.out.print("N ");
        return a = z;
    }
    public static void main(String [] args )
    {
        int b = 0;
        assert b > 0 : N(7);
        assert b > 1 : M(8);
        System.out.println("O ");
    }
}
output: O
```

```
class Test
{
    public static void main(String [] args)
    {
        Test p = new Test();
        p.method();
    }
    void  method()
    {
        long [] a = {20,30,40};
        long [] b = m(a);
        System.out.print(a[0] + a[1] + a[2] + " ");
        System.out.println(b[0] + b[1] + b[2]);
    }

    long [] m(long [] c)
    {
        c[1] = 10;
        return c;
    }
}
output: 70 70
```

```
class Test
{
    public static void main(String [] args)
    {
      int a = 0x80000000;
        System.out.print(a);
        a =a >>> 31;
        System.out.println(a);
        int i = 100;
        double c = 100.1;
        boolean d = (i == c);
        System.out.println(d);
    }
}
output: -21474836481 false
```

```
public class Test
{
    public static void main(String [] args)
    {
        try
        {
            method();
            System.out.print("A");
        }
        catch (Exception ex)
        {
            System.out.print("B");
        }
        finally
        {
            System.out.print("C");
        }
        System.out.print("D");
    }
    public static void method()
    {
        throw new Error();
    }
}
output: CException in thread "main" java.lang.Error at Test.badMethod(Test.java:22) at
Test.main(Test.java:7)
```

```
public class Test
{
    public static void main(String [] args)
    {
        try
        {
            method();
            System.out.print(" 1");
        }
        catch (RuntimeException ex)
        {
            System.out.print(" 2");
        }
        catch (Exception ex1)
        {
            System.out.print(" 3");
        }
        finally
        {
            System.out.print(" 4");
        }
        System.out.print(" 5");
    }
    public static void method()
    {
        throw new RuntimeException();
    }
}
output: 2 4 5
```

```
class Test
{
    public static void main(String args[])
    {
        Test h = new Test();
        System.out.println(h.method());
    }
    Object method()
    {
        Object o = new Object();
        Object [] obj2 = new Object[1];
        obj2[0] = o;
        o = null;
        return obj2[0];
    }
}
output: Java.lang.Object address.
```

```
class A { }
class Test
{
    A method()
    {
        A b = new A();
        return b;
    }
    public static void main (String args[])
    {
        Test t = new Test();
        A a = t.method();
        System.out.println("a");
        a = new A();
        System.out.println("b");
    }
}
output: A B
```

```
public class Test
{
    public static void main(String[] args)
    {
        try
        {
            int y = 0 / 0; ;
        }
        catch(Exception e){
         e.printStackTrace();
        }
        finally
        {
            System.out.println( "A" );
        }
    }
}

output: java.lang.ArithmeticException: / by zero at Test.main(Test.java:7) A
```

```
public class Test
{
    public static void main(String [] args)
    {
        Boolean a = new Boolean("true");
        boolean b;
        b = a.booleanValue();
        if (!b)
        {
            b = true;
            System.out.print("1");
        }
        if (a & b)
        {
            System.out.print("2");
        }
        System.out.println("3");
    }
}
output: 23
```

```
class Test
{
    public static void main(String [] args)
    {
        Test s = new Test();
        s.s();
    }

    void s()
    {
        int i = 5;
        int j = 8;
        System.out.print(" " + 2 + 4 + " ");
        System.out.print(i + j);
        System.out.print(" " + i + j + " ");
        System.out.print(m() + i + j + " ");
        System.out.println(i + j + m());
    }

    String m()
    {
        return "Hi";
    }
}
output: 24 13 58 Hi58 13Hi
```

```
class Test
{
    boolean [] a = new boolean[13];
    int c = 0;

    void set(boolean [] x, int i)
    {
        x[i] = true;
        ++c;
    }

    public static void main(String [] args)
    {
        Test ba = new Test();
        ba.set(ba.a, 1);
        ba.set(ba.a, 2);
        ba.m();
    }

    void m()
    {
        if ( a[0] && a[1] | a[2] )
            c++;
        if ( a[1] && a[(++c - 2)] )
            c += 7;
        System.out.println("c = " + c);
    }
}
output: c=10
```

```
class Test implements Runnable
{
    int a, b;
    public void run()
    {
        for(int i = 0; i < 1000; i++)
            synchronized(this)
            {
                a = 1;
                b = 2;
            }
        System.out.print(a + " " + b + " ");
    }
    public static void main(String args[])
    {
        Test run = new Test();
        Thread t1 = new Thread(run);
        Thread t2 = new Thread(run);
        t1.start();
        t2.start();
    }
}
output: 1 2 1 2
```

```
public class Test
{
    public static int b;
    public static int m(int a)
    {
        System.out.print("A ");
      return  b = a;
    }
    public static int n(int z)
    {
        System.out.print("B ");
        return b = z;
    }
    public static void main(String [] args )
    {
        int t = 0;
        assert t > 0 : n(7);
        assert t > 1 : m(8);
        System.out.println("C ");
    }
}
output: C
```

```
public class Test
{
    public static int a;
    public static int m(int b)
    {
        return b * 1;
    }
    public static void main(String [] args)
    {
        int c = 2;
        assert c > 0;
        assert c > 1: m(c);
        if ( c < 5 )
            assert c > 4;

        switch (c)
        {
            case 4: System.out.println("A");
            case 5: System.out.println("B");
            default: assert c < 6;
        }

        if ( c < 6 )
            assert c > 4: c++;
        System.out.println(c);
    }
}
output: 2
```

```
public class Test
{
    public static void main(String [] args)
    {
    String str = "12";
        try
        {
            str = str.concat(".1");
            double b = Double.parseDouble(str);
            str = Double.toString(b);
            int a = (int) Math.ceil(Double.valueOf(str).doubleValue());
            System.out.println(a);
        }
        catch (NumberFormatException e)
        {
            System.out.println("Exception !");
        }
    }
}
output: 13
```

```
public class Test
{
    public static void stringReplace (String txt)
    {
        txt = txt.replace ('a' , 'b');
    }
    public static void bufferReplace (StringBuffer txt)
    {
        txt = txt.append ("c");
    }
    public static void main (String args[])
    {
        String str = new String ("abcd");
        StringBuffer txt = new StringBuffer ("abcd");
        stringReplace(str);
        bufferReplace(txt);
        System.out.println (str + txt);
    }
}
output: abcdabcdc
```

```
public class Test
{
    public static void main(String [] args)
    {
      float a[ ], b[ ];
        a = new float[5];
        b = a;
        System.out.println("b[0]=" + b[0]);
    }
}
output: b[0]=0.0
```

```
class A
{
    byte b;
}

class Test
{
    public static void main(String [] args)
    {
        Test p = new Test();
        p.start();
    }

    void start()
    {
        A a = new A();
        System.out.print(a.b + " ");
        A a2 = m(a);
        System.out.println(a.b + " " + a2.b);
    }

    A m(A tt)
    {
        tt.b = 11;
        return tt;
    }
}
output: 0 11 11
```

```
public class Test
{
    static boolean b1, b2;
    public static void main(String [] args)
    {
        int x = 0;
        if ( !b1 )
        {
            if ( !b2 )
            {
                b1 = true;
                x++;
                if ( 1 > 2 )
                {
                    x++;
                }
                if ( !b1 )
                    x = x + 2;
                else if ( b2 = true )
                    x = x + 1;
                else if ( b1 | b2 )
                    x = x + 2;
            }
        }
        System.out.println(x);
    }
}
output: 2
```

```
public class Test
{
    static boolean a;
    public static void main(String [] args)
    {
        short s = 11;
        if ( s < 11 && !a )
            s++;
        if ( s > 11 );
        else if ( s > 10 )
        {
            s += 2;
            s++;
        }
        else
            --s;
        System.out.println(s);
    }
}
output: 14
```

```
public class Test
{
    public static void main(String [] args)
    {
      double m = -9.0;
        System.out.println( Math.sqrt(m));
        String a = ""+Math.sqrt(m);
        System.out.println(a);
        a = a.substring(0,1);
        char b = a.charAt(0);
        a = a + b;
        System.out.println(a);
    }
}
output: NaN NaN NN
```

```
public class Test
{
    public static void main(String [] args)
    {
        int r = 0;

        Boolean bool1 = new Boolean("TRUE");
        Boolean bool2 = new Boolean("true");
        Boolean bool3 = new Boolean("tRuE");
        Boolean bool4 = new Boolean("false");

        if (bool1 == bool2)
            r = 1;
        if (bool1.equals(bool2) )
            r = r + 1;
        if (bool2 == bool4)
            r = r + 10;
        if (bool2.equals(bool4) )
            r = r + 100;
        if (bool2.equals(bool3) )
            r = r + 1000;
        System.out.println("r = " + r);
    }
}
output: r = 1001
```

```
class Test extends Thread
{
    final StringBuffer s1 = new StringBuffer();
    final StringBuffer s2 = new StringBuffer();

    public static void main(String args[])
    {
        final Test t = new Test();

        new Thread()
        {
            public void run()
            {
                synchronized(this)
                {
                    t.s1.append("1");
                    t.s2.append("2");
                    System.out.println(t.s1);
                    System.out.println(t.s2);
                }
            }
        }.start();

        new Thread()
        {
            public void run()
            {
                synchronized(this)
                {
                    t.s1.append("3");
                    t.s2.append("4");
                    System.out.println(t.s2);
                    System.out.println(t.s1);
                }
            }
        }.start();
    }
}
output: 1 2 24 13
```

```
class Test extends Thread
{
    public static void main(String [] args)
    {
        Test t = new Test();
        Thread a = new Thread(t);
        a.start();
    }
    public void run()
    {
        for(int i = 0; i < 2; ++i)
        {
            System.out.println(i);
        }
    }
}
output: 0 1
```

```
public class Test
{
    public static void main(String [] args )
    {
        int r = 0;
        Test t = new Test();
        Object o = t;

        if (o == t)
            r = 1;
        if (o != t)
            r = r + 1;
        if (o.equals(t) )
            r = r + 10;
        if (t.equals(o) )
            r = r + 100;
        System.out.println("r = " + r);
    }
}
output: r = 111
```

```
public class Test
{
    public static void main(String[] args)
    {
        String str = "foo";
        Object obj = (Object)str;
        if (str.equals(obj))
        {
            System.out.print("1");
        }
        else
        {
            System.out.print("2");
        }
        if (obj.equals(str))
        {
            System.out.print("3");
        }
        else
        {
            System.out.print("4");
        }
    }
}
output: 13
```

```
public class Test
{
    static int q;
    static void m(int p)
    {
        boolean a;
        do
        {
            a = p<10 | m1(1);
            a = p<10 || m1(2);
        }while (!a);
    }
    static boolean m1(int p)
    {
        q += p;
        return true;
    }
    public static void main(String[] args)
    {
        m(0);
        System.out.println( "q = " + q );
    }
}
output: q = 1
```

```
public class Test
{
    public static void main (String [] args)
    {
        Thread th = new Thread()
        {
            Clz m = new Clz();
            public void run()
            {
                System.out.println( m.method(22));
            }
        };
        th.start();
    }
}
class Clz
{
    private int d = 11;
    public int method(int a)
    {
        int x = d;
        return d = x + a;
    }
}
output: 33
```

```
class A { }
class B extends A { }
class C extends A { }
public class Test
{
    public static void main (String [] args)
    {
        A a = new B();
        if( a instanceof B )
            System.out.println ("B");
        else if( a instanceof A )
            System.out.println ("A");
        else if( a instanceof C )
            System.out.println ( "C" );
        else
            System.out.println ("D ");
    }
}
output: B
```

```
class A extends Exception { }
class B extends A { }
public class Test
{
    public static void main(String args[])
    {
        try
        {
            throw new B();
        }
        catch (A a)
        {
            System.out.println("A");
        }
        catch (Exception e)
        {
            System.out.println("B");
        }
    }
}
output:B
```

```
public abstract class Test
{
    public int method()
    {
        return 22;
    }
    public abstract class B
    {
        public int method()
        {
            return 33;
        }
    }
    public static void main (String [] args)
    {
        Test t = new Test()
        {
            public int method()
            {
                return 44;
            }
        };
        Test.B b = t.new B()
        {
            public int method()
            {
                return 55;
            }
        };

        System.out.println(b.method() + " " + t.method());
    }
}
output: 55 44
```

```
public class Test implements Runnable
{
    private int a;
    private int b;

    public static void main(String [] args)
    {
     Test t = new Test();
        (new Thread(t)).start( );
        (new Thread(t)).start( );
    }
    public synchronized void run( )
    {
        for (;;)
        {
            a++;
            b++;
            System.out.println("a = " + a + " b = " + b);
            if(a==b)
             break;
        }
    }
}
output: a = 1 b = 1 a = 2 b = 2
```

```
class Test extends Thread
{
    public static void main(String [] args)
    {
        Test t = new Test();
        t.run();
    }

    public void run()
    {
        for(int i=1; i < 5; ++i)
        {
            System.out.print((i!=i) + " ");
        }
    }
}
output: false false false false
```

```java
public class Test extends Thread
{
    public void run()
    {
        System.out.println("A");
        yield();
        System.out.println("B");
    }
    public static void main(String []argv)
    {
        (new Test()).start();
    }
}
output: A B
```

```java
public class Test implements Runnable
{
    private int a;
    private int b;

    public static void main(String args[])
    {
        Test t = new Test();
        (new Thread(t)).start();
        (new Thread(t)).start();
    }
    public synchronized void run()
    {
        for(int i = 0; i < 4; i++)
        {
            a++;
            b++;
            System.out.println("a = " + a + ", b = " + b);
        }
    }
}
output: a = 1, b = 1 a = 2, b = 2 a = 3, b = 3 a = 4, b = 4 a = 5, b = 5 a = 6, b = 6 a = 7, b = 7
a = 8, b = 8
```

```
public class Test
{
    public static void main(String [] args)
    {
        int r = 0;
        short s = 5;
        Long a = new Long("5");
        Long b = new Long(5);
        Short c = new Short("5");
        Short a1 = new Short(s);
        Integer b1 = new Integer("5");
        Integer c1 = new Integer(5);
        if (a == b)
            r = 1;
        if (a.equals(b) )
            r = r + 1;
        if (a.equals(c) )
            r = r + 10;
        if (a.equals(a1) )
            r = r + 100;
        if (a.equals(c1) )
            r = r + 1000;
        System.out.println("r = " + r);
    }
}
output: r = 1
```

```
class Test
{
    public static void main(String[] args)
    {
        int a = 1;
        int b = 2;
        String str = "A";
        System.out.println(a + b + str);
        String str1 = "ABC";
        String str2 = "DEF";
        String str3 = str2;
        str2 = "GHI";
        System.out.println(str1 + str2 + str3);
    }
}
output: 3A ABCGHIDEF
```

```
class A
{
    A()
    {
        System.out.print("A");
    }
}
public class Test extends A
{
    public static void main(String[] args)
    {
        new Test();
        new A();
    }
}
output: AA
```

```
public class Test extends A
{
    public static void main(String [] args)
    {
        Test t = new Test();
        t.method();
    }
}
abstract class A
{
    void method()
    {
        for (int a = 0; a < 5; a++,a++ )
        {
            System.out.print(" " + a);
        }
    }
}
output: 0 2 4
```

```java
import java.util.Vector;
class A extends Vector
{
    int i = 1;
    public int ABC()
    {
        return (i=2)*i++;
    }
}
public class Test extends A
{
    public Test ()
    {
        i = 3;
    }
    public static void main (String args [])
    {
        A a = new Test();
        System.out.println(a.ABC());
    }
}
output: 4
```

```java
public class Test
{
    public int m()
    {
        static int j = 0;
        j++;
        return j;
    }
    public static void main(String args[])
    {
        Test t = new Test();
        t.m();
        int k = t.m();
        System.out.println(k);
    }
}
output: Exception in thread "main" java.lang.Error: Unresolved compilation problem:
Illegal modifier for parameter j; only final is permitted at Test.m(Test.java:5) at
Test.main(Test.java:12)
```

```
public class Test
{
    public static void main(String args[])
    {
     try
     {
         Float a = new Float("5.0");
         byte b = a.byteValue();
         int c = a.intValue();
         double d = a.doubleValue();
         System.out.println(c + b + d);
     }
     catch (NumberFormatException e)
     {
         System.out.println("Exception");
     }
    }
}
output: 15.0
```

```
public class Test
{
    public static void main(String[] args)
    {
     String str = "Hi";
     Object obj = str;
     String str2= new String("Hi");
     if( obj.equals(str) )
     {
         System.out.println("A");
     }
     else
     {
         System.out.println("B");
     }
     if( str.equals(obj) )
     {
         System.out.println("C");
     }
     else
     {
         System.out.println("D");
     }
     if( str2==str )
     {
         System.out.println("A");
     }
     else
     {
         System.out.println("B");
     }
     if( obj==str )
     {
         System.out.println("C");
     }
     else
     {
         System.out.println("D");
     }
    }
}
output: A C B C
```

18.3 PHP APTITUDE

```php
<?php
$var .= "1";
$var .= "2";
$var .= "3";
echo $var;

$var += "a";
$var += "b";
$var += "c";
echo $var;
?>
```

Output:
123123
Explanation: It does string concatenation if you use '.' operator.

```php
<?php
$var1 = array("var1" => "A", "var2" => "B");
$var2 = array("var1" => "C", "var2" => "D", "c" => "E");

$c = $var1 + $var2;
echo "Union of \$var1 and \$var2: \n";
var_dump($c);

$c = $var2 + $var1;
echo "Union of \$var2 and \$var1: \n";
var_dump($c);
?>
```

Output:
Union of *var1and*var2: array(3) ["var1"]=¿ string(1) "A" ["var2"]=¿ string(1) "B" ["c"]=¿ string(1) "E" Union of *var2and*var1: array(3) ["var1"]=¿ string(1) "C" ["var2"]=¿ string(1) "D" ["c"]=¿ string(1) "E"
Explanation: Here, values and keys of arrays are compared and printing the result.

```php
<?php
$var = 3;
$c=0;
for ($i = 0; $i <= $var; $i++) {
$a[$c++] .= "a";
}
echo var_dump($a);
?>
```

```
Output:

array(4) {
  [0]=>
  string(1) "a"
  [1]=>
  string(1) "a"
  [2]=>
  string(1) "a"
  [3]=>
  string(1) "a"
}
```

```php
<?php
echo 'Variable type checking...';
$a = 1.1;
$b = 2;
$c = "3";
$d = '4';
$e = array(1,2);
$f = array(1.1,2.2);
echo gettype(a)."\n";
echo gettype(b)."\n";
echo gettype(c)."\n";
echo gettype(d)."\n";
echo gettype(e)."\n";
echo gettype(f)."\n";
echo 'Array value type checking...';
$arr = array(2, 1.1, NULL, new stdClass, 'abc');
foreach ($arr as $val) {
    echo gettype($val), "\n";
}
?>
```

```
Output:

Variable type checking...string
string
string
string
string
Array value type checking...integer
double
NULL
object
string
```

Explanation:*gettype* is used to check the type of the PHP variable. The possible returned values of *gettype* are boolean, integer, double, string, array, object, resource, NULL and unknownType.

```php
<?php
$var = '1';
$var1 = &$var;
$var1 = "2$var";
echo $var1."\n";
$var2 = '123';
$var3 = substr($var2, 0, -1);
echo $var3 ;
?>
```

Output:
21 12

```php
<?php
 echo var_dump((string)(int)false);
 echo var_dump((string)(int)TRUE);
 echo var_dump((string)(double)(int)FaLsE);
?>
```

Output:
string(1) "0"
string(1) "1"
string(1) "0"

```php
<?php
$name = "ABC";
$$name = "DEF";
print "$name{$$name} \n";
print "$name$$name \n";
echo  "$name{$$name} \n";
echo "$name$$name \n";
System.out.print($name{$$name})."\n";
System.out.print($name." ".$$name);
?>
```

Output:

ABCDEF
ABC$ABC
ABCDEF
ABC$ABC
A
ABC DEF

```php
<?php
$var1 = "A";
$var2 = "B";
echo ${$var1$var2};
echo ${$var1 . $var2} = "Check1";
echo $AB;
echo $var1$var2;
?>
```

Output:

PHP Parse error: syntax error, unexpected '$var2' (T_VARIABLE) in /home-/ety2BJ/prog.php on line 4

Explanation:You can construct a variable name by concatenating two different variables but $$var1$var2 is not allowed.

```php
<?php
$var1 = "var2";
$var2 = '$var1';
echo $var2."\n";
$var1 = array("a","b","c");
$i=0;
foreach ($var1 as $var2){
echo $var1[$i++].$var2."\n";
}
?>
```

Output:

```
 $var1
aa
bb
cc
```

Index

www.ingramcontent.com/pod-product-compliance
Lightning Source LLC
Chambersburg PA
CBHW060528060326
40690CB00017B/3424